Development Centre Studies

Privatisation in Sub-Saharan Africa

Where do we stand?

Edited by

Jean-Claude Berthélemy, Céline Kauffmann,
Marie-Anne Valfort, Lucia Wegner

OECD

DEVELOPMENT CENTRE OF THE ORGANISATION
FOR ECONOMIC CO-OPERATION AND DEVELOPMENT

ORGANISATION FOR ECONOMIC CO-OPERATION AND DEVELOPMENT

Pursuant to Article 1 of the Convention signed in Paris on 14th December 1960, and which came into force on 30th September 1961, the Organisation for Economic Co-operation and Development (OECD) shall promote policies designed:

- to achieve the highest sustainable economic growth and employment and a rising standard of living in member countries, while maintaining financial stability, and thus to contribute to the development of the world economy;
- to contribute to sound economic expansion in member as well as non-member countries in the process of economic development; and
- to contribute to the expansion of world trade on a multilateral, non-discriminatory basis in accordance with international obligations.

The original member countries of the OECD are Austria, Belgium, Canada, Denmark, France, Germany, Greece, Iceland, Ireland, Italy, Luxembourg, the Netherlands, Norway, Portugal, Spain, Sweden, Switzerland, Turkey, the United Kingdom and the United States. The following countries became members subsequently through accession at the dates indicated hereafter: Japan (28th April 1964), Finland (28th January 1969), Australia (7th June 1971), New Zealand (29th May 1973), Mexico (18th May 1994), the Czech Republic (21st December 1995), Hungary (7th May 1996), Poland (22nd November 1996), Korea (12th December 1996) and the Slovak Republic (14th December 2000). The Commission of the European Communities takes part in the work of the OECD (Article 13 of the OECD Convention).

The Development Centre of the Organisation for Economic Co-operation and Development was established by decision of the OECD Council on 23rd October 1962 and comprises twenty-two member countries of the OECD: Austria, Belgium, Canada, the Czech Republic, Denmark, Finland, France, Germany, Greece, Iceland, Ireland, Italy, Korea, Luxembourg, Mexico, the Netherlands, Norway, Portugal, Slovak Republic, Spain, Sweden, Switzerland, as well as Chile since November 1998 and India since February 2001. The Commission of the European Communities also takes part in the Centre's Governing Board.

The purpose of the Centre is to bring together the knowledge and experience available in member countries of both economic development and the formulation and execution of general economic policies; to adapt such knowledge and experience to the actual needs of countries or regions in the process of development and to put the results at the disposal of the countries by appropriate means.

The Centre is part of the "Development Cluster" at the OECD and enjoys scientific independence in the execution of its task. As part of the Cluster, together with the Centre for Co-operation with Non-Members, the Development Co-operation Directorate, and the Sahel and West Africa Club, the Development Centre can draw upon the experience and knowledge available in the OECD in the development field.

 THE OPINIONS EXPRESSED AND ARGUMENTS EMPLOYED IN THIS PUBLICATION ARE THE SOLE RESPONSIBILITY OF THE AUTHORS AND DO NOT NECESSARILY REFLECT THOSE OF THE OECD OR THE GOVERNMENTS OF THEIR MEMBER COUNTRIES.

*
* *

Publié en français sous le titre :
Privatisation en Afrique subsaharienne
UN ÉTAT DES LIEUX

© OECD 2004

Foreword

The African Economic Outlook project, which led to this volume, is a joint enterprise between the OECD Development Centre and the African Development Bank, supported financially by the European Union. Each annual AEO carries a central theme based upon original analysis and research carried on by local correspondents trained under the auspices of the AEO project and by experts from both institutions. This book, financially supported by the Swiss authorities, is based upon the 2002/2003 AEO theme.

Table of Contents

Preface

Privatisation is a key element is the reform agenda of developing countries. In Africa, as elsewhere, governments have begun to privatise, but these recent policies are, to a large extent, unfinished. In addition, they are still being debated and consensus is yet to emerge, especially around their social implications.

There is a particular need today to examine privatisation programmes in Africa, at a moment when privatisation of public services, considered to be strategic sectors, are underway or in preparation, and when there has been so little in-depth analysis of the privatisation policies being pursued on the continent. One reason for the lack of analysis is the shortage of information, whether it be data on privatised enterprises or more qualitative details of the methods employed or planned to be used to disengage the state.

In the context of the preparation of the annual, joint African Development Bank/OECD Development Centre African Economic Outlook, the Centre brings together and analyses the principal economic data on a wide range of African countries in order to establish a regular diagnosis of the economic and social situations of these countries. This is an ideal way to produce well-documented comparative analysis of the policies being followed on the continent. For the 2002/2003 edition, published in March 2003, special attention was given to analysis of privatisation as a response to questions raised by earlier work for the AEO. This publication is a natural extension to this analysis.

A major reason for resistance from large sections of national and international public opinion to privatisation in Africa stems from the fear that privatisation hurts the poor. The debate is flawed, however, because, while it is easy to highlight the ending of subsidies linked to privatisation policies, it is as difficult to evaluate with any precision the fiscal impact because of the lack of transparency in the financing of public enterprises in Africa. Often, it is only the generally minimal income from the sales of public companies that is publicised, while savings to the budget from such divestment remain undisclosed. As a result, the enhanced room for manoeuvre produced by privatisation for spending on poverty alleviation may be underestimated. Whether or not governments do, in fact, use the extra resources for combating poverty, obviously depends upon their policy choices other than those relating to privatisation, especially since these extra resources are not clearly identified and evaluated at the time of privatisation.

Another aspect of the problem is that public enterprises can supply services at reduced prices, thanks to their subsidies, and privatisation can increase poverty by raising prices or reducing supply. Here, also, the argument can be biased if all the information is not considered. In the first place, it is rare that the poorest people have access to the goods and services supplied by public enterprises – especially public utilities. Further, privatisation can also – and that is one of its objectives – lead to improved productive efficiency which should lead to cost reduction and an increase in supply.

This publication highlights several examples of successful privatisation in Africa according to these criteria. None the less, there are also failures, particularly in the case of public utilities. This happens when privatisation has not been preceded by the creation of a regulatory framework to ensure that contractors or bidders respect their undertakings made at the time of privatisation and obliges them to maintain a competitive environment. Underlying all this, however, is the presence or absence of good governance on which successful privatisation reposes. In a context of good governance, at a time of privatisation the authorities can strengthen their initiatives in the struggle against poverty through transparent, participative and equitable public policy. The examples of success and failure documented in this book demonstrate that the key to success can be found in reinforcing the national authorities' ownership of the privatisation process. This requires considerable political will on the part of governments and strong capacities for implementing the reforms within the public sector.

Louka T. Katseli
Director, OECD Development Centre
January 2004

Executive Summary

Privatisation is a much-debated topic in both developed and developing countries, as it calls into question the role of the state in modern economies. In Africa, it is a rather recent phenomenon that began in Côte d'Ivoire in 1960, but accelerated dramatically in the 1990s under pressure from the Bretton Woods institutions. As of today, thirty-eight countries in sub-Saharan Africa have already implemented privatisation programmes, following closely the privatisation pattern initiated in the OECD countries in the mid-1980s in terms of sectors targeted: while most privatisations of small and medium-sized enterprises in the competitive sector took place in the early 1990s, it was only in the second half of the 1990s that the process started to involve larger enterprises, including, in recent years, companies in the network utilities sector. The similitude between the two regions obviously stops there, as they began privatising for different reasons: the OECD countries were seeking to reduce production costs in a context of stagnating demand, while the African countries were aiming to increase supply and raise immediate revenue for the government through the sale of assets.

Need for a Greater In-depth Study

Although useful research has already been devoted to privatisation in the African context (notably Campbell and Bhatia, 1998; Makalou, 1999, 2001; and Nellis, 2003), the issue needs deeper analysis for two main reasons. First, available data is sketchy, and most studies rely on very partial information, making the constitution of a sound database an essential preliminary step to any assessment of the divestiture process. Second, the discussion of the African privatisation process needs to draw on the lessons from recent experiences in order to highlight the necessary conditions and the ways to overcome obstacles to implement a successful privatisation. Assessing the outcome of privatisation is a complicated task, however, owing not only to the lack of reliable data but also, and more importantly, to the recent implementation and multi-dimensional nature of the divestiture process. In the African context, the debate is further complicated by the priority given to poverty reduction. The outcome of privatisation must therefore be assessed not merely in terms of its impact on economic efficiency but also in terms of social welfare (and the underlying issue of political stability) and longer-term aspects such as the development of local capacity.

Such an analysis is particularly necessary in the case of network utilities, because the privatisation of power, water, transport and to some extent telecommunications enterprises raises sector-specific issues, owing to the strategic nature of such firms: they are large; they provide both production inputs and crucial elements of household consumption; they substantially determine the well-being of the population; and they are an essential tool of distributive policy making, since they can be used by politicians to support either progressive policies (with tariffs far below actual costs, at least for lower-income consumers) or, in contrast, clientelist objectives (by granting privileges to civil servants, e.g. through overstaffing). Owing to the possibility of economies of scale and important sunk costs, network utilities also display very specific features in terms of organisation, naturally leading to market concentration. This "natural monopoly" status means that their privatisation has a very substantial distributional impact on consumers, since it strongly influences tariffs, output and access.

This study builds on an existing World Bank database, completed by authors' calculations and research aimed at filling the gaps in the information and detecting the misreporting of data. Based on that database, the book provides a broad picture of the size, the evolution, the sectoral breakdown and the methods of privatisation processes in Africa up to end 2002. Based on this dataset, the privatisation process implemented so far in Africa is assessed in the light of four objectives of privatisation, as viewed from the standpoint of the respective potential beneficiaries:

i)   First, the study discusses the budgetary objective of privatisation from the viewpoint of the state. It investigates both the direct, immediate effect of privatisation on fiscal revenues, through flows of sale proceeds, and the indirect, long-term effect stemming from cuts in subsidies, fewer bailouts of indebted state-owned companies and increased tax revenue.

ii) Then, viewing privatisation from a market angle, the improvement in economic efficiency generated by the change of ownership is evaluated.

iii) Thirdly, the results of divestiture in the network utility sectors in terms of prices and access are assessed from the consumer angle.

iv) Finally, from a macroeconomic point of view, the study examines whether African stock markets have benefited from privatisation and in general if privatisation has led to the development of the local private sector.

A review of case studies in sub-Saharan Africa reveals that, the ultimate question, which is transversal to all the above mentioned dimensions, is whether the process has benefited the poor. Depending on the existence of a regulatory framework and the government commitment in implementing privatisation policies, the impact of privatisation on poverty may vary widely. Overall, compared with other regions, the sub-Saharan Africa privatisation process has proceeded at a much slower pace and is still incomplete. We attempt below to provide some elements to understand the limited outcome so far of privatisation in Africa. We then highlight some key findings of the study, focusing on the possible outcomes of privatisation policies on poverty.

Privatisation in Sub Saharan Africa: Bottlenecks Encountered in the Process

Overall, the reasons for the limited results compared to the ambitious agenda of privatisation lie in the difficulties encountered in preparing for and implementing the process. In the first place, time is required to design a proper regulatory framework to guarantee a smooth transition. In many instances, the privatisation programme also suffers from the incompetence of the privatisation agencies appointed. In others, vested interests played a major role in retaining the so-called "strategic companies" in the hands of the state, leading to the postponement of the privatisation plan. The reluctance of governments to sell companies in some vital sectors of the economy and in the utilities sector often resulted in neglect of the economic situation of SOEs, which became increasingly unproductive, inefficient, overstaffed and characterised by bad management and corruption. Postponement of privatisation accompanied by the deteriorating situation of some SOEs led local and foreign investors to adopt a wait-and-see attitude, which ultimately exacerbated governments' difficulties in attracting potential investors.

Public opinion is another important reason for the postponement of many privatisation policies. The general hostility of the public has been based on fear of employee layoffs, price increases and the perception that the benefits and the distributional impact of privatisation are long in coming. In many countries, the commencement of the privatisation process has led to riots and protracted political debate.

Privatisation Rationalises State Role and May Free Resources for Poverty Targeted Expenditure

Privatisation transactions are often considered detrimental to the poor because they entail the elimination of subsidies to products and services, such as water, electricity and public transportation. The question, however, is whether such goods and services are best subsidized through state involvement in their production.

Past history has proved that not all subsidies to SOEs are geared to reduce poverty, mainly because those who have access to the services concerned are the richest groups. In many instances, public enterprises have been used to secure rents to a relatively small clientele, offering either above-market wages or under-pricing for those with access. Even when significant rates of subsidies are applied on the official market, many poor people are forced to buy from secondary markets (due to lack of legal access), and the benefits of low official prices are also enjoyed by the rich.

On the other hand, public money saved through privatisation, may be invested in poverty targeted projects. What is achieved by privatisation is essentially a clarification of the role of the state. Consequently, governments and the international agencies supporting their reform programmes should make a greater effort to clearly identify the fiscal resources saved through privatisation, and to channel these resources to poverty-targeted expenditure. This is however not easily done without a clear evaluation of the net resources added to the budget through a privatisation transaction (including the proceeds of the sale, the elimination of subsidies and broadening of the tax base) and of the amount of subsidies the poor actually enjoyed before privatisation.

An Unclear Impact of Privatisation on Labour Market: Short Term Redundancies and Long Term Uncertainty.

Although difficult to assess, owing to the lack of accurate figures on pre- and post-privatisation employment, privatisation is generally perceived to lead to job cuts in the short run. This perception has caused massive protests by trade unions, leading to the most vehement opposition to privatisation.

The available evidence on employment, however, is less clear-cut. The restructuring of previously overstaffed SOEs generally leads to redundancies in the short run. The long-term impact is however uncertain. The evidence for competitive sectors suggests that after registering a sometimes significant decrease in the year of privatisation, employment generally stabilises and then begins to trend upward in the two years following the launch of a privatisation plan. In public utilities, however, large-scale retrenchments were even more widespread as the combination of considerable overstaffing and insufficient training to keep staff up to date seriously constrained efficiency gains. Consequently, job redundancies have been particularly severe in the electric power sector, while water mostly remained under strong public control.

To soften the impact on employment, some national authorities have become more attentive to job preservation during the privatisation process under public opinion pressure. In Zambia and Burkina Faso, for instance, the retention of existing staff became an explicit criterion with which private investors had to comply. In the case of the privatised water company of Guinea, employees have been redeployed in subcontractor companies. As a cushion against the negative social impact of job redundancies, some Southern African governments have negotiated severance packages in co-operation with companies and trade unions.

Regarding the remaining manpower in privatised companies, there is some evidence that privatisation has helped improved labour practices and led to increases in wages, as exemplified by the privatisation of CI-telecom in Côte d'Ivoire.

Privatisation and Prices: Regulation to Complement Competition

There is widespread concern that cuts in subsidies might be socially damaging because they lead to price increases. The evidence shows that such price increases are in fact highly dependent on the specific characteristics of the sector. In the case of telecommunications, prices may actually be pushed downwards because the change of ownership is often accompanied by increased competition, owing to the simultaneous granting of one or more mobile telephone licences and in some cases a second fixed licence. In contrast, privatisation in power and water has generally led to higher tariffs because the high sunk costs involved have constrained the liberalisation of these sectors. Moreover, since it had been common practice to subsidise electricity and water tariffs, many holders of concession and lease agreements have had to re-adjust tariffs to cost-recovering levels subsequent to privatisation. In many cases, tariffs have been raised before the actual privatisation in order to reduce the companies' financing gap and to attract strategic buyers.

In other cases, price increases have been attributable to badly monitored price regulation systems. One way of overcoming the problem of information asymmetry (where the regulator does not have accurate information on the costs of suppliers) has been the adoption of rules for concession and lease bidding under which only the bidder offering service at the lowest price may be selected.

It should be noted, however, that despite the adverse impact of tariff increases, consumers have generally benefited from improvements in quality after privatisation. The reduction of distribution and transmission losses and the elimination of blackouts and brownouts appear to have more than offset increases in prices.

Finally, some privatisation methods may actually be consistent with a policy of subsidisation if the provision of public services at a reasonable price cannot be fully profitable. In the utilities sector, this would require clear and enforceable concession contracts that commit the concessionaire to supply services for the poor in exchange for an explicit or implicit subsidy. In turn, of course, this requires a transparent privatisation procedure and the implementation of an enforceable regulatory framework.

Privatisation and Access: Private-Public Partnership to Tackle the Challenges of Bringing Services to the Poor

The evidence suggests that privatisation accompanied by proper regulation is also a valuable alternative to state management to ensure increased access for consumers and overall improvements in quality. The case of telecommunications is an outstanding example of how privatisation has improved the coverage of public services. In particular, the evidence shows that privatisation brings broader access when it is accompanied by the simultaneous introduction of competition and proper regulation.

A credible regulatory framework, backed by strong political commitment, is also crucial to improving access in the power and water sectors. In the absence of proper regulation, profit-maximising behaviour has led privatised companies to keep investments below the necessary levels, with the result that rural communities and the urban poor were further marginalised in terms of access to electric power and water supply. One way to overcome the difficulties linked to the marginalisation of certain categories of consumers would be to include, in the licences of concessionaires and private power distributors, specific targets for electrification of rural communities and poor urban neighbourhoods, which could be part of the minimum requirement for licence renewal. Another option that has proven to increase the electrification of rural communities and urban poor in developed countries is to sell off the distribution end in smaller entities rather than in its entirety.

However, increasing the number of households with access to public services implies massive investment, both in production capacity and in network extension. These are long-term investments, and their viability depends in part on households' capacity to pay. In order to enhance access and design strategies to extend services to the poor, it is necessary to understand how much consumers are actually willing to pay and the constraints they face (in terms of access to credit, for instance). What is needed is a comprehensive strategy to co-ordinate the policies and programmes through which micro-credit, technology uptake and capacity building can take place. The formation of a well-balanced partnership between private operators, the government, customers and international lenders may be instrumental in improving access for the poor.

In total, the African privatisation process is still far from complete, given that it actually started only recently, and that it has been facing significant opposition in some countries. This makes the present assessment all the more useful, as the lessons learnt from the past ten years of privatisation can be used to improve divestiture methods for the companies that remain to be privatised, which in a number of countries include some of the largest and most strategic companies. Moreover, the way privatisations are managed has a considerable impact on public opinion and the attitude it will take towards further privatisation experiences, and more generally towards any kind of structural adjustment programme. The outcomes of privatisation should thus be a leading concern of development economists and especially of international donors, who are the main instigators of privatisation programmes in African countries.

Introduction

Privatisation is a much-debated topic in both developed and developing countries, as it calls into question the role of the state in modern economies. In Africa, privatisation is a rather recent phenomenon. It began in Côte d'Ivoire in 1960, when the Ivorian government signed a concession contract with SAUR that led to partial privatisation of the water supply company SODECI, and accelerated dramatically in the 1990s under pressure from the Bretton Woods institutions. The privatisation process in Africa closely followed the process initiated in the OECD countries in the mid-1980s, adopting the same pattern in terms of sectors targeted: the process began with the sale of companies from the competitive sectors, then shifted towards the disposal of network infrastructure assets such as telecommunications, transport, power and water. Utilities still account for a substantial proportion of pending privatisation projects in most countries of sub-Saharan Africa[1]. The similitude between the two regions obviously stops there, as they began privatising for different reasons: the OECD countries were seeking to reduce production costs in a context of stagnating demand, while the African countries were aiming to increase supply and raise immediate revenue for the government through the sale of assets.

The aim of this study is to document the privatisation process in Africa and discuss its outcomes. The intent is neither to justify nor to reject privatisation, but rather, on the basis of past experience, to highlight key elements of both successful privatisations and failures. Although useful research has already been devoted to privatisation (notably Campbell and Bhatia, 1998; Makalou, 1999, 2001; and Nellis, 2003), it is worth discussing in greater depth in the African context, for two main reasons. First, available data on African privatisations are sketchy, and most studies rely on very partial information, making the constitution of a sound database an essential preliminary step to any assessment of the divestiture process. Second, some discussion of the African privatisation process that encompasses the lessons learnt from recent analytical research on the conditions of successful privatisation is badly needed, since the available material on Africa is essentially descriptive.

Such an analysis is particularly necessary in the case of network utilities, because the privatisation of power, water, transport and to some extent telecommunications enterprises appears to raise sector-specific issues, owing to the strategic nature of such firms: they are large; they provide both production inputs and crucial elements of household consumption; they largely determine the well-being of the population; and they are an essential tool of distributive policy making, since they can be used by politicians to support either progressive policies (with tariffs far below actual costs, at least for lower-income consumers) or, in contrast, clientelist objectives (by granting privileges to civil servants, e.g. through overstaffing). Owing to the importance of such firms for the general well-being, the way they are managed has a considerable impact on public opinion and the attitude it will take towards further privatisation experiences, and more generally towards any kind of structural adjustment programme. The outcomes of privatisation in network utilities should thus be a leading concern of development economists and especially of international donors, who are the main instigators of privatisation programmes in African countries.

Network utilities also display very specific features in terms of organisation. Owing to the possibility of economies of scale and important sunk costs, they naturally lead to market concentration. This "natural monopoly" status means that privatising them has a very substantial distributional impact on consumers, since it strongly influences tariffs, output and access.

The combination of natural monopoly status and strategic importance makes it necessary to use specific privatisation methods for the utilities sector. On the one hand, strong regulation is needed to ensure that their monopolistic position does not lead to inappropriate pricing and under-investment when utilities are sold off to profit-maximising private investors. On the other, it is now recognised that network utilities are not monolithic monopolies but include activities that might support competition. The "operating" segment of a monopolistic business is potentially the most profitable, and as such is the most easily divested, while infrastructure, which traditionally requires heavy investment, remains under state ownership and control. This raises the issue of the optimal "design" of contracts (concessions, leases etc.) between government and private investors. Such contracts should lead to proper risk sharing and thus create appropriate incentives to make privatisation coincide with substantial investment aiming at upgrading and extending network services. This volume discusses these issues in depth and shows that progress in the establishment of proper regulation is greatly needed in Africa.

Assessing the outcome of privatisation is a complicated task, however, owing not only to the lack of reliable data but also, and more importantly, to the recent implementation and multidimensional nature of the divestiture process. In the African context, the debate is further complicated by the priority given to poverty reduction. The outcome of privatisation must therefore be assessed not merely in terms of its impact on economic efficiency but also in terms of social welfare (and the underlying issue of political stability) and longer-term aspects such as the development of local capacity. Furthermore, in cases where the previous situation favoured limited but powerful segments of the population (e.g. civil servants or political elites), privatisation necessarily implies a split in society between the potential "winners" and the potential "losers". Under such conditions, we will regard "failed" privatisations as those cases where the losers largely outnumber the winners, and "successful" ones as those cases where the winners largely outnumber the losers.

This study builds on an existing World Bank database to give a broad picture of the size, the evolution, the sectoral breakdown and the methods of privatisation processes in Africa. A detailed description, based on accurate data, is a precondition for any assessment of whether and to what extent privatisation in Africa has been successful. However, this World Bank database provides only the company name, sector, privatisation method and proceeds for each privatisation transaction, and it covers only the years up to 1999. This makes it necessary to crosscheck the available information and to extend the coverage of the database through 2002. This study is therefore based on new estimates concerning privatisation, for which, in the interest of transparency, we provide all necessary information and assumptions.

The analysis in the first part of the volume, based on the completed database, shows that the African privatisation process did not become significant in terms of number of transactions and sale values until the second half of the 1990s. The cumulative proceeds of privatisation in Africa have remained small, totalling some $8.8 billion over the 1990-2000 period, as against $46 billion in transition economies[2] and $177 billion in Latin America and the Caribbean[3]. In terms of sectors, the competitive sectors still account for the bulk of privatisation operations, although many African countries have started to privatise public utilities, particularly in the telecommunications sector. The observed sequencing of privatisation — starting with the competitive sectors, then moving on to bigger entities — is largely due to the difficulties encountered in privatising utilities. It led us to focus on the issue of privatisation of network infrastructure assets.

The core of this volume is an attempt to assess the privatisation process implemented so far in Africa in the light of four objectives of privatisation, as viewed from the standpoint of the respective potential beneficiaries. First, taking the viewpoint of the state, the study discusses the budgetary objective. It investigates both the direct, immediate effect of privatisation on fiscal revenues, through flows of sale proceeds, and the indirect, long-term effect stemming from cuts in subsidies, fewer bailouts of indebted state-owned companies and increased tax revenue. Although the evidence is sketchy, the study provides some indications that the indirect fiscal gains of privatisation can be substantial, outweighing in some cases the direct proceeds that accrue to government.

Second, viewing privatisation from a market angle, we evaluate the improvement in economic efficiency generated by the change of ownership. Significant gains have been observed in the competitive sectors, but the gains have been less obvious in the utilities sectors, where mechanisms to regulate natural monopolies have rarely been properly implemented in Africa. A notable exception is the telecommunications sector, where the competition introduced by mobile phone companies has led to considerable efficiency gains. This analysis is supplemented by a discussion of the social consequences of efficiency gains, as privatisation very often entails redundancies and increased unemployment in the short term. The final outcome remains unclear, but the discussion highlights once again the need to distinguish between short-term and long-term effects.

Third, considering privatisation from the consumer angle, we investigate the results of divestiture in the network utility sectors in terms of prices and access. The distributional effect of privatisation remains a key issue, as utilities are crucial elements of both national consumption and production. Impacts on prices and access vary widely, according to the capacity of the sectors considered to sustain competition. Case studies suggest, however, that even when competition is successfully introduced, the regulatory framework remains a key determinant of access and quality improvements. We report a number of cases in Africa where privatisations failed due to poor governance and the absence of a sound regulatory framework.

Finally, from a macroeconomic point of view, privatisation is expected to promote the expansion of financial markets and support local empowerment. The study examines case studies in order to determine whether African stock markets have benefited from privatisation. The development of the local private sector is then analysed, based on a review of the major obstacles faced by local actors when trying to participate in the reform.

In contrast to the situation observed elsewhere, the African privatisation process is still far from complete, given that it did not actually start until recently, and that it has faced and still faces significant opposition in some countries. This makes the present assessment all the more useful, as the lessons learnt from the past ten years of privatisation can be used to improve divestiture methods for the companies that remain to be privatised, which in a number of countries include some of the largest and most strategic companies.

Notes

1. This sectoral pattern of privatisation differs from that found in Latin America, where 57 per cent of the companies privatised from 1986 to 1999 belonged to the utilities sectors.

2. Bulgaria, Czech Republic, Hungary, Poland, Russian Federation, Turkey.

3. Argentina, Bolivia, Brazil, Chile, Colombia, Peru, Venezuela.

Chapter 1

The Record So Far

The Database

The statistical analysis undertaken herein is based on the World Bank African Privatization Database and on the authors' calculations and research aimed at filling the gaps in the information and detecting the misreporting of data. The database has been updated up to 2002 (it initially covered the process from the beginning to 1999), with particular emphasis on privatisation in the utilities sector (power, water and telecommunications), using the questionnaires on privatisation collected on-site by the "African Economic Outlook" team of the OECD Development Centre, working in collaboration with the African Development Bank. The resulting database is intended to offer the most up-to-date possible overview of the privatisation process.

It covers the 48 sub-Saharan African countries — of which ten had not yet started a privatisation programme at the time of the survey — over the 1979-2002 period. It also provides information on pending privatisations, covering in all 2 867 transactions (2 535 actual privatisations, 332 pending). For each country, the database reports the years of the transactions, the companies concerned, their sector, the methods used, the state's ownership share before and after privatisation, and the sale values. The following table shows, country by country, the starting date of privatisation, the total number of transactions and the resulting proceeds. Further information on the compilation of the database, including a comparison with other existing privatisation databases and the methodology used to extrapolate the missing data, can be found in Annexes 1 and 2.

Table 1.1. **Privatisations in 48 African Countries by Date, Number and Proceeds**

Region	Country	Date of first privatisation	Total number of privatisations up to 2002	Pending privatisations as of March 2003	Total proceeds ($ million)
Central Africa	Burundi	1988	38	2	19.8
	Cameroon	1994	29	10	227.4
	Central African Rep.	1986	25	18	18.5
	Chad	1993	35	5	9.9
	Congo	1992	66	59	0
	Congo Dem. Rep.	1987	21		52.5
	Equatorial Guinea	None			
	Gabon	1997	8	14	65.2
	Rwanda	1997	4	4	4.2
	São Tomé & Principe	1989	6		3.4
Eastern Africa	Comoros	None			
	Djibouti	None			
	Eritrea	None			
	Ethiopia	1995	10	1	203.3
	Kenya	1992	187	4	248.9
	Madagascar	1984	65	49	49.7
	Mauritius	2000	1		261
	Seychelles	None	None		
	Somalia	None			
	Sudan	1992	33	8	111.4
	Tanzania	1992	202	2	554.3
	Uganda	1991	106	9	228.5
Western Africa	Benin	1986	37	10	43.8
	Burkina Faso	1992	28		26.1
	Cape Verde	1993	41	17	101.8
	Côte d'Ivoire	1979[a]	80	2	423.6
	Gambia	1987	19	3	13.6
	Ghana	1989	180		946.2
	Guinea	1985	109	13	80.7
	Guinea-Bissau	1989	23	8	5.6
	Liberia	None			
	Mali	1979	71	17	90.9
	Mauritania	1989	35	2	56.1
	Niger	1983	28	6	25.2
	Nigeria	1989	63	12	672.4
	Senegal	1986	36	14	217.1
	Sierra Leone	1993	8		0
	Togo	1984	60	19	103.9
Southern Africa	Angola	1996	56	1	33
	Botswana	None			
	Lesotho	1995	10		37.2
	Malawi	1989	46	12	57
	Mozambique	1986	487	7	324.1
	Namibia	None			
	South Africa	1996	14	2	2 510.1
	Swaziland	None	79	103.9	
	Zambia	1992	255	3	717.5
	Zimbabwe	1994	13	7	272.6
Total			2 535	332	8 816.2

a. The first privatisation in Côte d'Ivoire actually took place in 1960, but the database starts only in 1979.

Table 1.2. **Regional Distribution**

	Share in total GDP (%)	Share in total population (%)	Total number of countries	Countries that privatised		
				Number	Share of regional GDP (%)	Share of regional population (%)
Central Africa	9	14.5	10	9	93.6	99.5
Eastern Africa[a]	18	32.1	12	7	96.4	93.4
Western Africa[b]	26	33.7	16	15	100[c]	98.7
Southern Africa	47	19.7	10	7	93.1	96.8

a.   Including Sudan.
b.   Including Mauritania.
c.   GDP of Liberia not available.

To allow regional analysis, we computed aggregate data for four groups, using the African Development Bank (ADB) classification: Central Africa, Eastern Africa, Southern Africa and Western Africa. For the purposes of this study, the two sub-Saharan countries classified by the ADB in Northern Africa were reallocated to Eastern Africa (Sudan) and Western Africa (Mauritania). Consequently, Central Africa and Southern Africa each account for 21 per cent of the sample in terms of number of countries, while Eastern Africa accounts for 25 per cent and Western Africa 33 per cent. The distribution of population among the four regions follows a similar pattern, with Central Africa accounting for 14.5 per cent of the total population of sub-Saharan Africa, Southern Africa 20 per cent, Eastern Africa 32 per cent and Western Africa 34 per cent. Where the distribution of GDP is concerned, however, the picture is completely different: Southern Africa accounts for almost half of total GDP, Western Africa 26 per cent, Eastern Africa 18 per cent and Central Africa 9 per cent. In Central and Western Africa all countries but one have started privatising, whereas in Southern Africa and Eastern Africa 30 per cent and 58 per cent of countries, respectively, have not yet begun the process.

Privatisation Transactions to End 2002: Continental and Regional Approach

Continental Overview

Number of Transactions

The total number of privatisations in sub-Saharan Africa to end 2002 amounts to 2 535 transactions. The first countries that undertook the privatisation process belong to the French-speaking sub-Saharan regions. The very first privatisation transaction in Africa was conducted in Côte d'Ivoire: a concession contract in the water sector signed in 1960 between the Ivorian government and SAUR. In 1979 and 1982, two Malian companies in manufacturing industry (SEBRIMA) and trade (SCAER) were liquidated and restructured by the government. From 1983 to 1986, the prevalence of French-speaking countries in the privatisation process remained unchallenged, with transactions occurring in Madagascar, Mali, Niger, Togo, Guinea, Benin, the Central African Republic and Senegal. From 1987 however, the Portuguese- and English-speaking countries started to privatise, with six transactions recorded in Mozambique and two in Gambia, followed in 1989 by Nigeria (15 transactions), Ghana (six transactions), São Tomé & Principe and Guinea-Bissau (one transaction each). These countries began the privatisation process for budgetary reasons, seeking to raise immediate revenue for the government through the sale of assets and thus to overcome the state's inability to finance needed expenditures on new investment and/or maintenance. They were also driven by the need to remove subsidies to the utilities sector in order to release resources for other pressing public expenditure and to improve the performance of state-run utilities companies, which was characterised by high costs, inadequate expansion of access to services for the poor and/or unreliable supply.

At the end of 2002, only 11 sub-Saharan countries had not recorded any (or very few) privatisation transactions: Botswana, Comoros, Djibouti, Equatorial Guinea, Eritrea, Liberia, Mauritius, Namibia, Seychelles, Somalia and Swaziland. In the cases of Botswana, Mauritius and Namibia, the main state-owned enterprises (SOEs) were operating efficiently and did not constitute a drain on central government expenditures, and/or the state faced no significant problems with its fiscal balance. These countries have thus been under no pressure to privatise. Other countries, such as Eritrea, Liberia and Somalia, did not enjoy sufficient political stability to be able to undertake economic reforms.

Some of these countries, however, have recently launched privatisation programmes and started entering the privatisation process. Mauritius, for instance, initiated a partial privatisation of Mauritius Telecom in 2000, with France Télécom taking 40 per cent of the capital. The objective was to prepare for the liberalisation of the sector, which finally took place in early 2003 when the company was restructured. The recent adoption of a privatisation plan in Botswana was mainly motivated by the objective of promoting economic diversification and empowering the local private sector.

Figure 1. **Annual Number of Privatisations and Proceeds up to 2002**

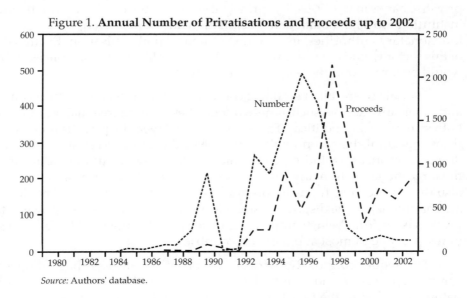

Source: Authors' database.

The donor community, particularly the World Bank and the IMF, has been very active in promoting privatisation. According to Ariyo and Jerome (1999), by the end of the 1980s a majority of African countries had received World Bank assistance for privatisation programmes and 67 per cent of all adjustment lending involved public enterprise reform. Harsch (2000) reports that by 1998, 34 African countries were under World Bank financing agreements that involved the privatisation process. Although privatisation was thus a cornerstone of the structural adjustment programmes initiated by the Bretton Woods institutions in the 1980s, the actual implementation of the process did not start until the early 1990s. This was mainly due to the fact that reform of SOEs was regarded as a second phase of structural adjustment, after the macroeconomic stabilisation programmes, being more demanding both politically (facing local opposition) and in terms of the implementation framework and actions involved (the need for a proper regulatory framework).

Indeed, as shown in Figure 1, it was not until the early 1990s that the number of privatisations per year increased significantly, after which it peaked at 495 privatisations in 1995 and gradually declined to the end of the period covered. Up to 1995, the emphasis was primarily on divesting small and medium-sized enterprises, which in most cases represented viable business ventures and were therefore more attractive to the private sector.

Another special case was that of the financial sector. In several African countries, bankruptcies in the sector made it necessary to liquidate, merge or privatise banks in the 1990s. The principal issue was the need to reform financial institutions so as to obtain better regulation and supervision of the sector by the monetary authorities, in a context of financial liberalisation. Examination of this sector would entail a discussion of financial liberalisation policies, which would be far beyond the scope of our study.

The sale of so-called strategic companies in vital sectors of the economy and in sensitive sectors such as network utilities encountered major difficulties, both structural and political. These obstacles delayed the privatisation of such firms: not until the second half of the 1990s did the process start to involve larger enterprises, including companies in the network utilities sector in the most recent years. In many cases, this shift in privatisation programmes was also due to pressure from the Bretton Woods institutions, which made their aid conditional on the disposal of sizeable assets. Nevertheless, the privatisation process is far from being complete, as major privatisations (332 in all) are still in the pipeline in most sub-Saharan countries.

The sequencing of the African privatisation process (beginning with competitive sectors and coming later to network utilities) closely follows the pattern initiated in the OECD countries in the mid-1980s, where the process also encountered public opposition and structural difficulties. In the OECD countries, however, the adoption of reforms was driven by stagnating demand and pressure to lower production costs in the context of the 1973 oil crisis, whereas the situation in the developing world was diametrically opposed, with very scarce and inefficient capacity leading to frequent shortages.

Sale Value

As an illustration of the peculiar sequencing of the privatisation process, Figure 1 shows that the distribution of sale values differs substantially from that of the number of transactions. The reason is that the first privatisations were numerous but yielded relatively little in the way of proceeds. In contrast, when it came to privatisation of utilities and strategic sectors of the economy, the process slowed down in terms of numbers but, initially at least, brought higher proceeds. Sale values declined towards the end of the period because the transactions occurring over the last three years mainly involved network utilities, and the proceeds from these sales have not been extrapolated in the database (with the exception of telecommunications). Thus, this decline may point to an underestimation problem in the database.

The total sale value to end 2002 is estimated at $8.8 billion. Figure 1 suggests that sale values follow a rising trend up to 1997 (when total sale proceeds reached $2.16 billion) and then gradually decline to $834 million in 2002 ($192 million when South Africa is excluded from the data). Since 2000, total sale values have amounted to only $2.2 billion ($1.5 billion excluding South Africa).

The peak in 1994 is mainly due to large privatisations in Ghana: the flotation of 25 per cent of the government's 55 per cent stake in the Ashanti Goldfields Corporation on the Ghana and London Stock Exchange, and the sale of the assets of the Ghana Consolidated Diamonds Corporation, the country's biggest diamond mining concern. The most spectacular peak occurred in 1997 with the sale of a 30 per cent stake in South Africa's telecom company Telkom; the value of the sale amounted to $1.26 billion, which explains the prominent place of South Africa in the privatisation process that year.

Best Performers

Comparison of the "Top 5" countries shows once again a lack of correlation between the number of transactions and the sale proceeds. It should be noted, however, that the recent focus on large firms has gradually led to a general increase in the average value[1] per transaction (see Figure 5).

Box 1. **Learning to Privatise**

Source: Kayizzi-Mugerwa, 2002

"**A. Stalemate** describes a position of minimal movement, with slow privatisation and a small volume of sales. This was the case for many African countries in the late 1980s, before the privatisation process achieved momentum. But owing to social strife and political difficulties, some countries have not moved far from here.

"**B.** The '**path of least resistance'** refers to a scenario, quite common in sub-Saharan Africa, where governments embarked on rapid privatisation of small firms, but baulked when it came to large companies. This was, for example, the experience of Zambia during the first five years of privatisation in the 1990s when close to 200 companies were divested and the government was praised by donors and multilateral agencies for undertaking one of the fastest and most transparent privatisations in Africa. The Zambian government claimed at the time that when it came to privatisation there were 'no sacred cows'. However, taken all together the companies sold thus far were only worth a fraction of the assets of Zambia Consolidated Copper Mines (ZCCM), the mining conglomerate, whose privatisation was long-drawn-out and controversial and was not completed until the end of the 1990s.

"Eventually, the stock of small firms in the 'path of least resistance' phase is exhausted and governments must resort to privatising larger ones. At about this time, the privatisation process begins to generate its own dynamics. This is partly a process of learning from earlier mistakes and strengthening the administrative and financial aspects of the process, including the introduction of new legal codes to remove loopholes.

"**C.** The third phase of privatisation can be referred to as **'breaking resistance'**. This characterised the bulk of sub-Saharan countries in the first half of the 1990s. At this stage, privatisation has been accepted in principle, and institutional and legislative means of implementing it are in place, but owing to institutional and political constraints — for example as symbols of national independence larger firms have considerable sentimental value in Africa — privatisation is much slower than before. The political mood is still against the divestiture of large companies. Some governments were able to privatise one or two large companies, for example, Kenya Airways in the mid-1990s and the electricity conglomerate CIE in Côte d'Ivoire in 1990. While often making little headway otherwise, the privatisation of a big company helps break resistance.

"**D.** The last phase, so far reached by only a few African countries, involves a **fully-fledged privatisation** effort, including firms formerly considered strategic in sectors such as telecommunications, electricity, water and other utilities. The phase is reached when political and institutional constraints on privatisation have been resolved, enabling rapid divestiture, with large companies coming on stream relatively quickly and with sales to foreigners causing little or no controversy. Under the fully-fledged privatisation phase governments have more experience and are able to make the necessary adjustments, notably with respect to strengthening the legal framework. Typically, the debate regarding the rationale for privatisation has at this stage been transcended, with the focus now on how the benefits of privatisation are allocated."

Figure 2. **Cumulated and Annual Sales Proceeds up to end 2002, Excluding South Africa**

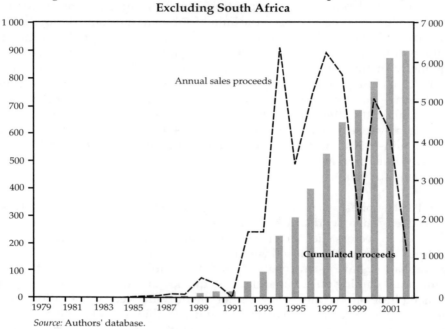

Source: Authors' database.

Figure 3. **Top 5 Countries by Number of Transactions**
(average relative value per transaction in millions)

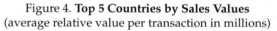

Ghana	$5.3 per transaction
Kenya	$1.3 per transaction
Tanzania	$2.7 per transaction
Zambia	$2.8 per transaction
Mozambique	$0.7 per transaction

Source: Authors' database.

Figure 4. **Top 5 Countries by Sales Values**
(average relative value per transaction in millions)

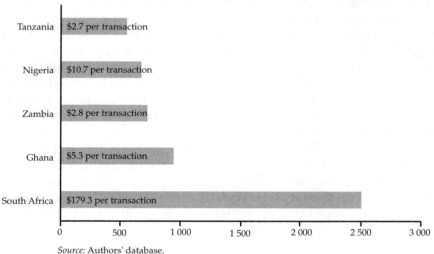

Tanzania	$2.7 per transaction
Nigeria	$10.7 per transaction
Zambia	$2.8 per transaction
Ghana	$5.3 per transaction
South Africa	$179.3 per transaction

Source: Authors' database.

Figure 5. **Average Value per Transaction in Sub-Saharan Africa over 1979-2002**
($ million)

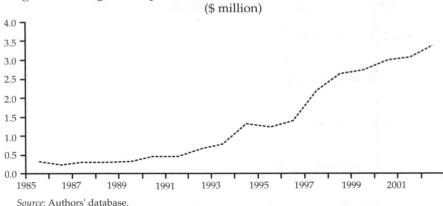

Source: Authors' database.

Although Mozambique ranks first in number of privatisations, the average value per transaction is only $0.7 million, excluding the $117 million granted by the donors to the authorities in 1999 for the sale of a 73 per cent stake in Aguas de Mozambique (ADM). Most privatisation operations in Mozambique thus far have involved small retail establishments, which explains why the country does not appear among the Top 5 in terms of sale value. Zambia, which ranks second in number of transactions, shows a per transaction value of only $2.8 million, and the latter value would be even lower if the recent privatisations in the mining sector had not been included. The high number of transactions in Zambia through the late 1990s is the result of the dismantling of large, non-core concerns in the residential housing sector into several small privatised units. As a result of these operations, thousands of Zambians have become homeowners through the sale of parastatal houses on favourable terms. Privatisation in these two countries, characterised by sales of residential housing or small commercial concerns, led in many cases to asset stripping. In Zambia, for instance, the 150 companies earmarked for privatisation were split up into about 300 units. According to the Technical Unit for Enterprise Restructuring, 1 248 companies have emerged from the privatisation process in Mozambique, while the World Bank reports only around 500 companies earmarked for it. Kenya follows a similar pattern, with a value per transaction amounting to only $1.3 million.

South Africa presents a peculiar case: the number of privatisations registered in the country is among the lowest in sub-Saharan Africa, and the total proceeds and average sale value are by far the highest. The main reason is that the privatisation process has thus far been largely focused on divestiture of the largest and most strategic SOEs: Eskom (electricity), Transnet (road, rail, maritime and air transport, including Spoornet, which runs the railways, and Portnet, which runs the seaport), Telkom (telecommunications) and Denel (defence). These four companies account for 91 per cent of estimated total assets, 86 per cent of turnover and 77 per cent of all employees in the top 30 SOEs[2].

Regional Performance

The yearly regional breakdowns of the numbers and sale values of privatisations in sub-Saharan Africa to end 2002 are reported in Figures 6 and 7.

Western and Southern Africa are the most dynamic zones in sub-Saharan Africa in terms of the number of transactions, accounting for 33 per cent and 32 per cent respectively of all privatisations to end 2002 (including pending transactions). Eastern Africa comes next with 23 per cent of registered transactions, and Central Africa lags far behind with 12 per cent. The ranking changes significantly, however, when the number of transactions is expressed in proportion to the number of countries in each region (with or without countries that have undertaken no privatisation): Southern Africa takes the lead, followed by Eastern Africa and only then by Western Africa. This is not surprising, since Mozambique and Zambia have been particularly active in terms of the number of privatisation transactions, as reported in Figure 3.

A similar pattern is observed regarding sale values. The dominant sub-region is again Southern Africa, which accounts for almost half of the total value of privatisation transactions to end 2002. This outstanding result is mainly due to the huge contribution of South Africa, which accounts for more than $2.5 billion; this figure represents two-thirds of total proceeds in Southern Africa, and nearly one-third of those reported for all sub-Saharan countries (see Figure 9). In terms of absolute numbers, Western Africa ranks second with one-third of total registered proceeds, but Eastern Africa shows a higher level of proceeds per country engaged in the privatisation process.

Central Africa lags well behind the other African sub-regions in terms of both total number of transactions and sale values. Within this region, the top ranking of the Republic of Congo (Brazzaville) should also be interpreted with caution since it refers not to significant transactions but rather to liquidations,

Figure 6. **Yearly Regional Distribution of Privatisation Transactions**

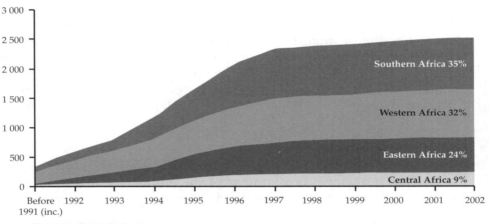

Source: Authors' database.

Figure 7. **Yearly Regional Distribution of Privatisation Proceeds, Highlighting South Africa in Southern Africa's Share**

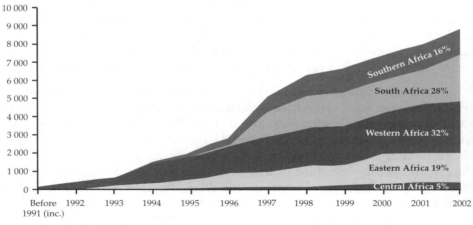

Source: Authors' database.

Figure 8. **Top 3 Countries in Each Sub-Saharan Region in Terms of Numbers**

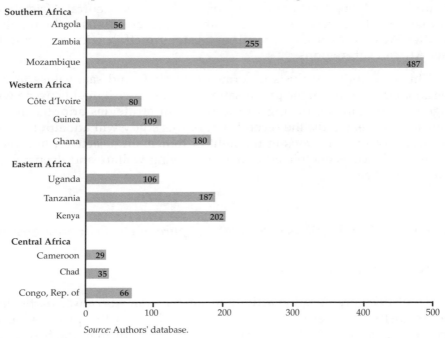

Source: Authors' database.

Figure 9. **Top 3 Countries in Each Sub-Saharan Region in Terms of Proceeds**

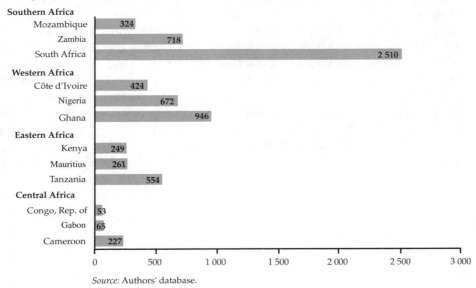

Source: Authors' database.

except for the sale of a 67 per cent stake in the telecom company for $50 million in 1996. As shown in Figure 10, however, Central Africa is the sub-region with the second largest number of privatisations in the pipeline, just after Western Africa, as a result of a catch-up effect with respect to the other African sub-regions.

This descriptive analysis in terms of numbers and sale values tells us little about the success of the privatisation process, since it might cover a wide range of situations according to the different strategies adopted by the countries. Consequently, the second part of this study will attempt to assess the success of privatisations in the light of four main objectives: improving the fiscal balance, economic efficiency, improving welfare and deepening of financial markets.

Privatisation Transactions to End-2002: Approach by Economic Sectors

Number of Transactions

Until 1998, privatisation activity in sub-Saharan Africa was particularly intense in the competitive sectors. Transactions in the primary sector (agriculture, agro-industry, forestry and fishery), in manufacturing and construction, and in tradable services (e.g. tourism and trade) account for nearly 70 per cent of the total number of privatisations recorded to end 2002. It should be noted, however, that many companies in the competitive sectors remain state-owned, whether earmarked for privatisation or not. This situation, which is peculiar to Africa, results from the pro-active development strategies adopted in many African countries during the first two decades after independence, when governments — including some regarded as market-oriented, as in Côte d'Ivoire — attempted to implement "big push" policies. Such policies were based in particular on active industrial policies, which led to the creation of SOEs in many competitive sectors. The decade of adjustment in the 1980s made it clear that such policies were building huge public or publicly guaranteed debt stocks, without much industrial development.

Figure 10. **Regional Distribution of Pending Privatisations**

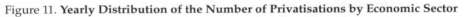

Southern Africa 10%

Central Africa 34%

Western Africa 36%

Eastern Africa 20%

Source: Authors' database.

Figure 11. **Yearly Distribution of the Number of Privatisations by Economic Sector**

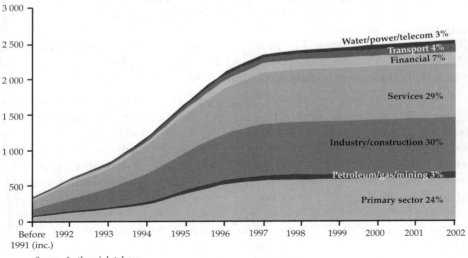

Source: Authors' database.

It is only recently that attention has moved to network utilities (power, water, telecom) and transport, which explains why only 7 per cent of the privatisations implemented so far have been in these sectors (and this figure drops to 3 per cent when transport is excluded). Another reason for the low percentage is that services in these sectors are usually provided by a unique incumbent operating as a monopoly.

Since 2000, privatisations in network utilities and transport have accounted for 30 per cent of the total number of transactions. These sectors also account for 30 per cent of pending projects in sub-Saharan Africa, with 46 companies soon to be privatised in water, power and telecommunications and 53 in transport. The bulk of pending transactions in the utilities sector will take place in telecommunications, with the planned privatisations of Camtel (Cameroon), Rwandatel (Rwanda), Socatel (Central African Republic), the Office National des Postes et Télécommunications (Chad) and Gabon Télécom. All the pending privatisations in the telecom, power and water sectors are listed in Annex 3.

This sequencing, which is also observed in other regions, reflects the special nature of these sectors and its impact on the privatisation process. Enterprises in the competitive sectors usually produce goods and services in response to the signals of free markets, with the result that such firms tend to be relatively small and to be numerous on the same market segment. In contrast, utilities produce strategic goods and services that are not only critical to the consumption of individuals, but also enter the national production process as inputs. Utilities are large entities, organised as monopolies owing to the size of the necessary infrastructure (in the water, power and fixed-line telephony sectors), which entails high sunk costs and the possibility of economies of scale.

Public ownership was at first seen as the best solution to avoid monopolistic pricing while resolving market failures and ensuring social welfare. Evidence from many sub-Saharan African countries suggests, however, that public ownership led instead to unproductive, inefficient and overstaffed public enterprises, characterised by bad management, under-investment and corruption. Corrupt and "clientelist" behaviour on the part of some governments has made it difficult to implement cost-covering prices and to undertake substantial investment. The result has been a considerable drain on fiscal balances and a decline in social welfare (through inadequate access to utilities, amplified by deficient and limited infrastructure, and through poor allocation of public expenditure). This situation induced the Bretton Woods institutions to propose privatisation, in the context of structural adjustment programmes, as the "solution" for governments facing such difficulties. The divestiture of utilities is a sensitive issue, however. As it entails difficult reforms, governments have frequently postponed such privatisations, and as a result this process is still in its early stages.

Figure 12. **Distribution of Pending Privatisations by Economic Sectors**

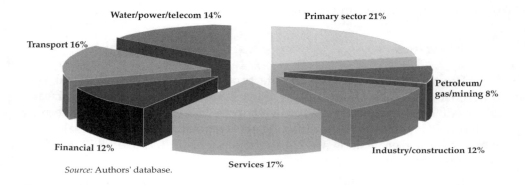

Source: Authors' database.

Figure 13. **Distribution of Privatisation Proceeds by Economic Sectors**

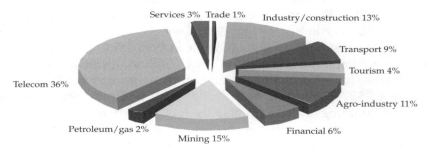

Source: Authors' database.

Utilities display particular characteristics that justify the use of specific privatisation methods. These methods are reviewed in the next section, "Privatisation Methods", with the emphasis on the approaches adopted in the case of the utilities under study.

Sale Values

The sectoral breakdown of sale proceeds to end 2002 leads to very different conclusions. Unfortunately, transaction values in the power and water sectors do not appear in Figure 13, owing to the lack of information concerning such privatisations and to the difficulty of extrapolating values in these sectors, where contract provisions are highly dependent on the overall state of the company considered.

Transactions in telecommunications account for only 1 per cent of the number of privatisation transactions, but more than one-third of the total sale value to end 2002 (mainly owing to the privatisation of Telkom in South Africa). This is more than the combined values of all transactions in the primary sector, manufacturing/construction and services. This finding confirms that privatisations in competitive sectors usually target small entities with generally low sale values. However, there are some exceptions. In the manufacturing/construction sector, for instance, one of the biggest transactions remains the competitive sale of a 51 per cent stake in the Tanzania Cigarette Company in 1995 for $55 million. Exceptions are also recorded in agro-industry, especially the sugar and rubber industries: in 1995, Côte d'Ivoire privatised its sugar company Sodesucre for $47.86 million, while in 1996 Cameroon sold the state-owned rubber company Hevecam for $32.43 million. In 2002, Ghana sold a 25 per cent stake in its Cocoa Processing Company through a public flotation amounting to $27.95 million. Sale values in the mining sector are also significant, accounting for 16 per cent of the total, with two major transactions in gold mining: the flotation between 1994 and 1996 of a 35 per cent stake in Ghana's Ashanti Goldfields Corporation amounting to $416 million, and the competitive sale of assets in 1998 of Lega Dembi Gold Mines in Ethiopia for $172 million. As regards Zambia Copper Mining, the transaction amounts show a considerable under-valuation of the assets sold, as the acquisition price in March 2000 was around $90 million, whereas the company's assets had been valued at $165 million two years earlier. Sale proceeds in the petroleum/gas sector are small primarily because privatisations have been undertaken in distribution activities rather than extraction. Moreover, only a few companies are in the business of gas distribution in sub-Saharan Africa, so little privatisation can be expected in the sector[3].

42

Figure 14. **Privatisation Methods**

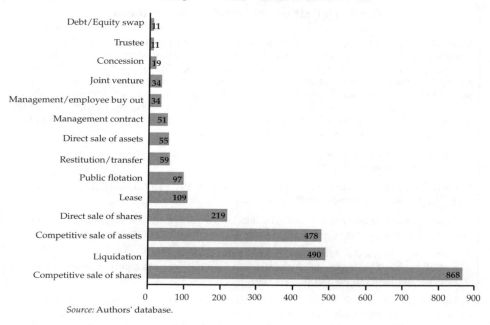

Source: Authors' database.

Privatisation Methods

Terminology

Overview of Privatisation Methods

The privatisation method used most often in sub-Saharan Africa has been the sale of shares (directly or through competition), followed closely by liquidations and sales of assets. Other methods are used much more rarely: leases, public flotation, transfers, management contracts, buyouts, joint ventures, concessions, trustees and swaps. Box 2 provides definitions of all these methods. In our analysis, we have made every effort to fill the gaps in our information about the methods used by updating systematically the reported transactions, using local as well as international sources.

Box 2. **Definitions of Privatisation Methods**[4]

Sales of shares and assets are the most commonly used privatisation methods in sub-Saharan Africa. They may be conducted through a competitive bidding process or through direct negotiations with one party. Privatisations through **"direct sales of shares/assets"** also include **"pre-emptive rights",** which refer to transactions whereby a government sells shares to existing private shareholders who exercise pre-emptive rights to acquire those shares in accordance with specific provisions of the company's charter. In some cases, the amount to be paid per share or the formula for calculating that amount is specified in the charter; otherwise, it becomes a matter for negotiation.

Other, less common methods include public flotation, management/employee buyouts, joint ventures, trustees and debt/equity swaps.

"Public flotation" refers to the sale of shares to individuals, financial institutions or private-sector businesses; the shares can then be traded on a stock market.

A **"management/employee buyout"** consists of the sale of the business to its managers and/or employees, giving them control of the future direction of the business.

Transactions described as **"trustees"** refer to privatisations effected by transferring shares in a public enterprise to a trustee for resale, at a later date or over a period, to the public or to selected segments of the public.

A **"debt/equity swap"** is a transaction in which a corporation exchanges equity against existing debt. A good illustration of a debt/equity swap occurred in Mali in 1994: the Chinese investors COVEC and CLETC acquired an 80 per cent stake in Comatex SA worth CFAF 1.2 billion ($1.69 million) and a 60 per cent stake in Sukala worth CFAF 3 billion ($4.23 million) in exchange for the reduction of Mali's debt to China by an equivalent amount.

A third set of methods, though reported as "privatisations", do not involve actual sale of government-owned shares or assets of public enterprises; rather, they involve reduction of the equity percentage held by government through share dilutions or transfer of enterprise assets. These methods are **liquidations**, **restitutions**, **joint ventures**, **leases**, **concessions** and **management contracts**.

Liquidations generally consist in the government's selling all of a company's assets and paying its outstanding debts, after which it goes out of business. Such transactions rarely lead to a return on capital (liquidated firms are generally highly indebted compared to the value of their assets). In some cases, however, the term "liquidation" refers rather to a **financial restructuring** of the company to pave the way for its future privatisation, as its value can be expected to appreciate following the reforms. Financial restructuring often means restructuring of the company's activities or corporate structure, usually combined with the liquidation of loss-making production facilities and the related sale of some corporate assets. Although such transactions are reported as "liquidations", they should be distinguished from the wholesale liquidation of a company's assets. Financial restructuring is generally preferred to wholesale liquidations because it allows creditors and shareholders to avoid the considerable expense, time and effort associated with the official liquidation of a bankrupt company, even giving them the possibility of some return on their capital in case of a future privatisation.

"Restitutions" are transactions whereby a company is returned to a previous owner from which it had been expropriated. We have grouped this method with **"transfers"**, in which the government donates an enterprise to local communities.

In a **"joint venture"**, a company owned jointly by the private and public sectors is set up to complete a project that benefits both parties. The remaining shell company can then be maintained only as a paper company or liquidated (in the latter case it is not counted as a liquidation, to avoid counting it twice).

Under a **"management contract"**, a private firm is appointed by the government to provide managerial services, often for a fixed fee.

A **"lease contract"** is a written agreement under which a property owner allows a tenant to use the property for a specified period of time and rent.

Under a **"concession agreement"**, the government specifies the rules under which the company can operate locally.

The last three types of contract (management contract, lease contract and concession agreement) are very common in the utilities sector and will be explored further in the next section.

To end 2002, the bulk of privatisations in Africa have been carried out through the competitive sale of shares (868) or assets (478). Direct sales of shares (219) are usually the result of shareholders' exercising their pre-emptive rights. Liquidations (or rather financial restructuring) are also a very frequently used method (490 transactions), if both total and partial sales of the company's assets are counted. Finally, privatisation through public flotation is little used: the 97 transactions reported represent only 3.8 per cent of all privatisations. Although such transactions have sometimes helped to "launch" capital markets in Africa, their infrequency shows that financial market development has not yet taken off in most African countries. This has considerably hampered the development of local ownership that was expected from the opening up of public access to dynamic stock markets, and it constitutes a major difference between privatisation in Africa and the privatisation process elsewhere, particularly in the OECD area.

Transactions involving an unambiguous sale or disposal of shares or assets thus account for 70 per cent of all recorded transactions (as against 22 per cent for liquidations and restitutions), while methods allowing government to keep some of its prerogatives are used in only 8 per cent of the total. As is discussed below, however, the supposedly "competitive" basis of most of the transactions in Africa appears to be very ambiguous and debatable. This may have reduced the efficiency of privatisation in Africa, as compared with other regions.

Figure 15. **Privatisation Methods in Sub-Saharan Africa to end-2002, by Sector**

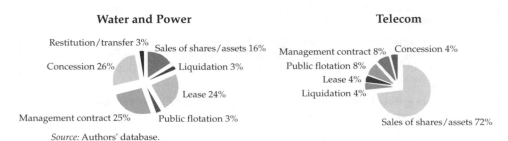

Source: Authors' database.

Utilities

Analysis of the sectoral breakdown of privatisation methods shows interesting results due to the distinctive character of the contracts signed between government and strategic investors in network utilities. The evidence suggests that the agreements most often used for divesting electricity and water companies are concessions, leases and management contracts (these methods are used in respectively 26, 24 and 25 per cent of all transactions). In telecommunications, competitive sales of shares account for 68 per cent of transactions. The different forms of participation offered to private investors in utilities are defined in Box 3, following Guislain and Kerf (1996). The differences between these options lie in the extent of the rights and obligations transferred to the private operator.

Management contracts are popular with investors because they allow the investing company to profit from the utility without the financial commitment required by full-scale privatisation. Such contracts may also offer investors a foothold in a utility that will give them an advantage if it is subsequently privatised. For example, the management contract signed between Chad's water and power company Société Tchadienne d'Eau et d'Electricité (STEE) and Vivendi in January 2000 made Vivendi the investor likely to be chosen when STEE is privatised, which is expected to take place by 2005.

Box 3. **Definition of the Participation Options Offered to Private Investors in Utilities**

Under a **subcontracting arrangement**, the private party is not directly responsible for providing public services but instead performs specific tasks, such as supplying inputs, construction, maintaining assets or billing customers, usually in exchange for a fixed fee. In the privatisation database, such subcontracting arrangements are not considered as privatisation transactions. As an example of such an arrangement, the Suez subsidiary Ondeo was awarded two contracts in Senegal to complete two water projects valued at a total of $32 million: the first consisted in building a pumping and water-purification plant in the town of Keur Momar-Sarr, at a cost of $15 million, and the second the construction of a water-purification plant in the town of Ziga at an estimated cost of $17 million.

Under a **management contract**, a private firm is appointed by the government to provide managerial services, often for a fixed fee. The contract typically requires the private party to manage a utility and provide services to the public for a given period of time. The remuneration of the private operator may be fixed at the outset, in which case the commercial risks of the operation are borne entirely by the public sector, or it may be linked to the performance of the utility, in which case the private operator bears some commercial risk. Management contracts are common practice in sub-Saharan Africa.

A **lease** is a written agreement under which a property owner allows a tenant to use the property for a specified period of time and a specified rent. The private-sector operator is responsible for providing the service at its own risk, including operating and maintaining the infrastructure for a given period of time. The operator is not responsible, however, for financing investment such as the replacement of major assets or expansion of the network. If payments from users cover more than the operator's remuneration, the operator is generally supposed to return the difference to the public authorities in order to cover the cost of the investments under the latter's responsibility. As an example, the British firm Biwater was reported in February 2002 to have been awarded a lease agreement to take over the national water company of the Congo, the Société Nationale de Distribution d'Eau (SNDE).

A **concession** is similar to a lease except that the private operator is responsible for asset replacement and network expansion as well. An example of a concession is the design, construction and operation of a sewage treatment plant in Durban (South Africa) by Vivendi. The term BOT (build-operate-transfer) is often used to refer to greenfield concessions. On expiration of a BOT, the assets are returned to the public sector. BOOs (build-own-operate) are similar to BOTs except that they do not involve transfer of the assets to the public sector after a pre-determined period of time. The private operator thus remains responsible for carrying out all the investment required to meet its service obligations. BOOs are the most common "concession" contracts used in the transport, water and power sectors (although contracts in the latter two are actually closer to *affermage* arrangements, as shown by the case of the French-speaking African countries). Under BOOT (build-own-operate-transfer) schemes, the private sector obtains the capital needed for construction, builds and operates the infrastructure for an agreed period of time (anywhere between 15 and 30 years) and then transfers ownership back to the relevant government. These schemes are becoming increasingly popular as a means of financing large-scale infrastructure development such as roads, bridges and hydro-electric dams.

Divestiture means that ownership of the existing assets and responsibility for future upkeep and expansion are transferred to the private sector. Divestiture is the method used in the privatisation of telecom and air transport concerns.

Source: Guislain and Kerf (1996).

Management contracts are also desirable from the standpoint of African countries since they can help to ensure a smooth privatisation process. The reason is that, although they entail no sale of shares, they usually lead to structural reforms in the sector that help the SOE concerned to become "profitable", making it considerably more attractive to potential investors once the actual privatisation is implemented. Such reforms also pave the way for a truly competitive tender process, which is known to facilitate subsequent regulation. Moreover, the period under private management usually helps to transfer know-how and entrepreneurial spirit to employees — a crucial point in Africa, where the lack of know-how among local investors constitutes a major obstacle to private-sector development. In Zambia, for instance, most small and medium-sized enterprises, although privatised quite easily, encountered major difficulties once on the market and went bankrupt owing to a lack of managerial capacity. Finally, management contracts appear to be an effective way of giving the government and the private investor time to build a tight partnership and thus make privatisation more successful in the event that the company under management contract is actually granted a majority stake in the firm.

Examples and distinctive features of lease and concession contracts are detailed below in the sub-section on privatisation in the power and water sectors, since divestiture in these sectors has mainly relied on such methods.

The Privatisation Process in Utilities

Given the special nature of utilities, their privatisation displays specific characteristics that are worth emphasising.

First, regardless of the type of network utility considered and the method used, the divestiture of the former SOE is always partial; the state retains a part of its stake, although it generally sells a majority share to the private investor, as shown in the tables below. Leroy *et al.* (2002) mention four possible reasons for the fact that governments prefer partial privatisation in these sectors:

Strategic: As mentioned above, utilities are often seen as too crucial to the national welfare to be entirely sold off to the private sector

Political: The population regards utilities as national property. A complete transfer of ownership to foreigners is therefore highly unpopular, as it calls into question both the identity and the sovereignty of the country. Such nationalist feelings are exacerbated by the colonial past of the countries under study, as the sale of strategic sectors to the former colonial power is seen as an attempt at re-colonisation.

Bureaucratic control: Partial privatisation allows the state to maintain some control over the sector.

Economic: Partial privatisation allows the state to retain some assets of the company and sell them later at a better price.

In the case of natural monopoly sectors such as water and power, there is a fifth reason: the need for further regulation of such sectors after their partial divestiture so as to prevent abusive behaviour on the part of the private investor, especially concerning tariffs and access. This explains why the sale of a majority stake in the "operating" company (the state usually retains ownership of the infrastructure) always coincides with the signature of a lease or concession contract that is supposed to lay down clear rules by which both the regulator and the operator must abide. The next sub-section, on privatisation in the water and power sectors, explores this issue further through a case study of urban water supply in Conakry and Abidjan.

A second distinctive feature of the privatisation of network utilities is that, at the demand of international donors, these transactions must be conducted on a competitive basis, as competition is deemed to generate higher sale proceeds and stronger incentives for competitors to disclose their operating costs. When this is not the case, and when the Bretton Woods institutions detect a blatant lack of transparency, uncompetitive transactions can lead to a straightforward suspension of donor funding programmes. In Ghana, for example, a contract awarded to Enron subsidiary Azurix for a BOOT water project was cancelled in 2002 after the World Bank withheld a $100 million funding programme because the contract had been awarded in unclear circumstances. Enforcing competition in privatisation deals is also naturally in the interest of African countries, and companies promoting uncompetitive bidding processes are sometimes prosecuted by national authorities. In Lesotho, subsidiaries of a dozen multinationals (from the United Kingdom, France, Italy, Germany, Canada, Sweden and Switzerland) have been prosecuted for paying bribes to obtain contracts in the Lesotho Highlands project (a water supply scheme).

The degree of real competition in the tender process is very questionable, however, since, owing to the huge investments required in the utilities sector, private investors are generally multinationals. As shown by the following tables, out of a total of 17 transactions, six have been concluded with SAUR, four with Vivendi, three with Suez, two with Biwater and two with Aguas de Portugal. Given that French firms sometimes operate as partners in sub-Saharan Africa, the extent of real competition becomes even more questionable.

Moreover, corruption is far from being systematically condemned, which can explain the less than satisfactory outcome of some privatisation experiences in the sector of infrastructure and network utilities. To take the case of infrastructure, the privatisation of Benin's petroleum marketing company SONACOP (Société Nationale de Commercialisation des Produits Pétroliers) led to a great scandal in 1999. According to the media, not only was the choice of the strategic local investor imposed by President Kerekou, but the investor acquired the company for free, since more than $26 million of its own assets were used for the purchase.

Even when the bidding process is ostensibly competitive, it sometimes bears a considerable resemblance to a straightforward "direct sale of shares or assets" because of bidding conditions that considerably restrict participation. The privatisation of Air Tanzania is a striking example of limited competition. Initially, eight airlines expressed interest in becoming strategic partners in Air Tanzania Corporation Limited (ATCL): South African Airways (SAA), Kenya Airways, the South African airlines Comair and Nationwide, Gulf Air Falcon of the United Arab Emirates, Aero Asia International of Pakistan, Air Consult International of Ireland and Precision Air of Tanzania. Of these eight, only four — SAA, Kenya Airways, Comair and Nationwide — went through the due diligence process, and on the bidding deadline in September 2002, only SAA submitted a bid. The others withdrew their interest in the deal, making the process much less competitive than expected. Such ambiguity regarding the actual competitiveness of the bidding process is not uncommon.

Not all utilities display exactly the same characteristics, however, and hence distinct privatisation methods are required. While energy and water are clearly public goods that require strong regulation to ensure both suitable prices and adequate access, certain segments of the telecommunications industry are viable commercial services that would benefit from open competition. The case of privatisation in these two sub-sectors is explored below.

Privatisation in Telecommunications

Privatisation in the telecommunications industry usually takes the form of partial divestiture through competitive sale of shares, but, in contrast to the power and water sectors, this is rarely followed by the signature of "regulatory" contracts such as concession or lease agreements (with the exception of the privatisation of CI-Telecom in 1997, which combined the sale of a 49 per cent stake to France Télécom with a 20-year concession contract). This is mainly due to technological advances (e.g. GSM technology and the Internet) that allow competition and thereby transform the telecommunications industry from a natural monopoly into a competitive sector. Indeed, according to the International Telecommunication Union (ITU), 30 countries in sub-Saharan Africa had more mobile than fixed telephones in 2001.

The regulatory framework thus appears to be far less crucial in the telecom sector than in the power and water sector, as the regulatory role is increasingly played by competition, which automatically forces telecom operators to reduce their prices (and thus their costs) and to extend their networks through investment (so as to win market share). As noted by Smith (1997), telecommunications has changed from a static, single-product, monopolistic industry to a dynamic, multi-product, multi-operator industry that is extremely open to technological progress and therefore much better able to cope with competition. It clearly follows that, if regulation is still necessary at all, the regulatory agenda has shifted from minimising the price of subscribing to local telephone services or maintaining cross-subsidies to managing multiple issues related to competition, entry, pricing and cross-subsidies. However, regulation by government agencies has become less necessary in telecommunications and may partly disappear in the long run in favour of multi-sector antitrust agencies.

As Smith points out, this does not mean that regulation no longer has a role to play. On the contrary, it is still greatly needed to protect consumers from, for instance, monopoly abuses resulting from collusion between operators. Furthermore, some segments of the telecommunications sector remain difficult to open to competition, as they either are unattractive to the private sector or require strong regulation to ensure that they develop properly. For instance, local telephony may not be a big enough market to ensure a profit for a private company. Similarly, a telecom company may not give priority to developing fixed-line infrastructure, being more interested in quick profits under the minimum investment conditions allowed by mobile telephony.

Privatisation in the Power and Water Sectors

In contrast to privatisation in telecommunications, partial divestitures in the power and water sectors have been conducted under a more specific contractual framework, principally relying on lease and concession contracts. As Sheshinski and López-Calva (1998) point out, concessions generate "competition for the market" when "competition in the market" is not feasible.

Table 1.3 **Privatisation in Telecommunications**

Country	Company	Year	Method (% sold)	Main strategic investor(s)	Comments
Cameroon	Camtel Mobile	2000	Lease (95)	Mobile Telephone Network (South Africa)	This transaction was a competitive sale combined with a 15-year lease contract.
Cape Verde	Cabo Verde Telecom	1995, 1996, 1999	Competitive sale of shares (86.6)	Portugal Telecom	Portugal Telecom: 40% National Social Prov. Institute: 27.9% Other domestic private sector: 13.7% State of Cape Verde: 13.4%; Employees: 5%
Central African Republic	Socatel	1990	Competitive sale of shares (40)	France Câble & Radio	Pending sale of the remaining 60%
Republic of Congo	Office National des Postes et Telecommunications (ONPT)	1996	Competitive sale of shares (67)	US Atlantic Tele Network	Pending sale of the remaining 33% (of which 5% to an employee shareholding scheme). The telecom company was renamed Société d'Exploitation des Télécommunications.
Côte d'Ivoire	Côte d'Ivoire Telecom	1997	Concession (49)	France Câble & Radio	This transaction is a competitive sale combined with a 20-year concession agreement, granting CI-Telecom a monopoly over land-based communications for a non-extendable period.
Ghana	Ghana Telecommuncations	1997	Competitive sale of shares (30)	G-Com, an 85%-owned subsidiary of Telekom Malaysia	In 2002/2003, a three-year management contract was signed with Telecom Management Partner (TMP), a wholly owned subsidiary of the Norwegian telecommunications group Telenor ASA, in charge of installing at least 400,000 fixed lines within three years. This followed the non-renewal of the five-year management contract signed with Telekom Malaysia along with the sale of the 30% share in 1997.
Guinea	Sotelgui	1995	Competitive sale of shares (60)	Consortium led by Telekom Malaysia	Telekom Malaysia subsequently reduced its stake to 30%.
Guinea-Bissau	Guiné Telecom	1989	Competitive sale of shares (51)	Portugal Telecom	Negotiations are currently under way with Portugal Telecom for an increased stake.
Lesotho	Lesotho Telecom	2000	Competitive sale of shares (70)	Consortium led by Zimbabwe's Econet Wireless International	Pending sale of the remaining 30% to local investors (of which 5% to an employee shareholding scheme)
Mauritius	Mauritius Telecom	2000	Competitive sale of shares (40)	France Télécom	Privatisation undertaken to restructure the company and prepare it for the liberalisation that took place early 2003.
Niger	Sonitel	2001	Competitive sale of shares (64)	ZTE Corporation China Right Company	ZTE Corporation China Right Company: 51%; National private investors: 11%; State: 34% Employees: 3%; France Câble & Radio: 0.89%
Nigeria	Nitel	2003	Management contract	Pentascope International	

Country	Company	Year	Method (% sold)	Main strategic investor(s)	Comments
São Tomé & Principe	Companhia Santomense de Telecommunicacoes (CST)	1989	Direct sale of shares (51)	Marconi (now merged with Portugal Telecom)	Private sale
Senegal	Sonatel	1997, 1998	Competitive sale of shares (33.3)	France Télécom	France Télécom's ownership share was increased to 42 per cent through a recapitalisation in 1999. At the time of the original sale, 10 per cent of the shares were sold to Sonatel employees at a highly discounted rate. Another 17 per cent were then offered in 1998 for public sale through the regional stock exchange BRVM; two-thirds were reserved for Senegalese nationals and institutions. All shares were quickly bought up; purchasers included some 9 000 Senegalese individuals who paid a total of CFAF 17 billion ($30 million).
South Africa	Telkom	1997	Competitive sale of shares (33)	SBC Communications:18% Telekom Malaysia:12% Johannesburg Stock Exchange: 3% (black empowerment)	15 per cent of the remaining shares were listed on the Johannesburg Stock Exchange on 4 March 2003.
Sudan	Sudatel	1994, 2001	Competitive sale of shares (50)	A wide range of private investors	It is listed on the Khartoum Stock Exchange and has an authorised capital of $250 million. In 2001, Sudatel became the first non-GCC (Gulf Cooperative Council) company to be listed on the Bahrain Stock Exchange. It is also the first Sudanese company to be listed on a stock market outside Sudan.
Tanzania	Tanzania Telecommunications Company	2000	Competitive sale of shares (35)	MSI (Netherlands)/Detecon (Germany) consortium	In February 2001, MSI/Detecon paid the first tranche of $60 million, but the second tranche due on 31 December 2001 was not paid, owing to a controversy over the soundness of TTCL's financial statements. In June 2002, the government finally decided to give back the first tranche of $60 million to MSI/Detecon as its share in the recapitalisation of TTCL.
Uganda	Uganda Telecom	2000	Competitive sale of shares (51)	A consortium led by the International Telecommunication Union's Investment Fund, WorldTel, and the Deutsche Telekom subsidiary Detecon	The consortium was the sole bidder in an international tender.

Source: Authors' calculations, based on various sources.

matter of fact, concessions are best suited for privatising sectors with monopolistic characteristics, as they allow the state to retain some control over the sector by stating clearly in a contract the terms and conditions under which the private-sector concern, selected through a competitive bidding process, is to run the company and to what extent it is responsible for investment.

Another way to help the government attract private investors in network utilities such as electricity and water is to design contracts under which the private firm acquires an interest only in the service delivery aspects of the utility (the "operating" activities), with the aim of making relatively quick profits, and leaves the financially less attractive responsibilities — typically the infrastructure — under the government's management. Such contracts, widely used in sub-Saharan Africa, are very similar to what in French is called *affermage*, a mix of lease and concessions. The weight of each of these aspects in the final deal depends on how the risks are shared between the private investor and the government. Concessions entail more risk for the former because they give private investors full responsibility for some or all investment. *Affermage* contracts are specific to French-speaking countries such as Senegal, Guinea, the Central African Republic and Côte d'Ivoire. They are management contracts that include the granting of a lease (with concession elements in some cases) to a private enterprise (which acquires a stake in the "operating" company) to run a system for a period of years. In contrast to straight management contracts, the concessionaire receives all the revenues and bears all operating costs, and usually enjoys a greater degree of freedom to determine the commercial strategy. *Affermage* contracts are usually concluded for long terms (up to 20 years) and are consistent with continued public ownership of assets and with price regulation. Finally, they often lead to the creation of what Kerf (2000) calls "state holding companies", which are wholly state-owned entities. State holding companies have been set up in Guinea, Senegal, the Central African Republic and Gambia.

The benefits of such contracts are evident. As the private investor generally acquires a majority stake in the most profitable part of the business when the lease or concession agreement is signed, it is supposed to have strong incentives to generate and secure revenue, even when it must abide by price regulation rules imposed by the government. Moreover, since the concessionaire is generally not responsible for very large investments (which remain the responsibility of the public authorities), it is easier for the regulator to evaluate the real operating costs of the private firm so as to create good price-setting mechanisms.

Box 4. The *Affermage* Contract and State Holding Companies

Private operators are responsible for the following tasks:
i) operating and maintaining the distribution network (the water distribution system in most cases, as only one *affermage* contract has been reported so far in the electricity sector);
ii) collecting revenues from users (and sharing these revenues with public entities); and,
iii) in some cases, carrying out some investment (i.e. some replacement of assets and network expansion).
The public authorities retain responsibility (often through a "state holding company") for:
i) designing sector policies and strategies;
ii) ownership of infrastructure assets;
iii) planning and financing some or all investment;
iv) regulating the activities of the private operator; and
v) promoting public acceptance of the Private Participation in Infrastructure (PPI) reforms.

Source: Kerf (2000).

These contracts also have a number of drawbacks, however. The continued public role in asset provision and heavy investment, combined with the long-term aspect of the contract, can lead to disequilibria in terms of risk sharing that, though attractive for the private investor, do not provide the right incentives for cost reduction, and hence for efficiency gains. Another problem can arise from the division of the former incumbent into two activities with different ownership: unless the contract clearly states the roles and responsibilities of the different parties, it can lead to great confusion between the public and private operators that is likely to increase the information asymmetry and can ultimately lead to inefficient regulatory mechanisms, high prices and under-investment. The regulatory structure for water in Côte d'Ivoire is a good illustration of the ambiguity of an *affermage* contract.

In July 1988, a new 20-year contract for the water sector took effect in Côte d'Ivoire. Whereas previously the responsibility for planning and financing investment was shared between two public entities (the Direction de l'Eau, or DE, and the Fonds National de l'Hydraulique), under the new contract the planning function was transferred to SODECI (which already had responsibility for operation and maintenance of all urban systems, including metering, billing and collection from all private- and public-sector customers). It was also decided that investment would be self-financed as much as possible. Consequently, the contract gave SODECI some control over investment along with its planning responsibilities, but SODECI bears no investment-related risk, as financing for investment is supposed to be generated by the difference between consumers' payments and the lease fees. These resources are channelled to the Fonds de Développement de l'Eau (FDE), which funds investment expenditures and is also responsible for "social connections" for low-income consumers, and to the Fonds National de l'Eau (FNE), which finances debt service. From 1995, however, SODECI's responsibility for investment execution increased: it was allowed to implement investments of less than $220 000 without going through a tender process. The new contract also reduced SODECI's remuneration, under the threat that the public authorities might allow other companies to bid for the contract. This reduction not only increased the funding available for investment but also led to lower water tariffs. Finally, the former "take or pay" provisions were eliminated from the new contract, again under the threat of contracting out. Before the reform, SODECI's remuneration had been based on the DE forecast of water sales, and when actual sales were lower than projected, SODECI was entitled to compensation. Under the new contract, SODECI's compensation was based upon the amount actually collected.

The impact in terms of investment and tariff decreases (or rather reduction in operating costs) has been mixed. The new contractual arrangement has led to a more efficient investment policy and a reduction in investment spending, whereas before the reform the DE had inappropriately over-invested in large production facilities at the expense of the distribution network. This subsequently led to an improvement in the rate of coverage (especially in Abidjan). However, the contract between the Ivorian authorities and SAUR was criticised for its mixture of concession and lease features, which allowed the private operator to undertake most investments without bearing the financial burden or the risk. This led Ménard and Clarke (2000) to analyse the respective advantages and drawbacks of concession and lease contracts in an environment like that of Côte d'Ivoire (see Box 5).

Box 5. **Water Privatisation in Côte d'Ivoire: Advantages and Drawbacks of Concession and Lease Contracts**

"The fundamental advantage of a **concession** is that it makes the firm fully responsible for investment, management and debt for the duration of the contract. Since profits depend upon its capacity to collect bills, the operator has a strong incentive to extend the network and to meter and bill users. However, unless certain conditions are fulfilled, concessions can be inefficient. *First*, the contract should be awarded through competitive tender. However, the uncertainties associated with running a water utility in a developing country mean that this is not always easy to do. Further, competition is likely to be even less effective for contract renewals, since the incumbent has a significant informational advantage. In Africa, because of the small number of firms that have been actively involved in the urban water sector, it is even more difficult to ensure that bidding is competitive. *Second*, the contractor's obligations (e.g., investment and network development) should be well specified, and easy to implement and monitor. Again, this can be difficult in developing countries, since many factors that affect the optimal evolution of the system are unpredictable (e.g., unplanned urban developments). *Third*, because water systems are close to a natural monopoly, there is a risk that the operator would continuously pressure for renegotiations, once the contract has been allocated. Hence, dispute resolution mechanisms must be well defined and efficient, which requires especially sophisticated and credible institutions. *Fourth*, the regulator monitoring the concession needs to have access to, and the technical ability to assess, relevant information (e.g., on costs and the maintenance of the system). Therefore, the contract needs to have adequate information revealing schemes and the regulator needs to have the technical and managerial skills to assess this information. *Fifth*, the firm might overuse equipment and under-invest in maintenance, particularly towards the end of the contract, if there is a risk that it will not have the contract in the next period. The only way to avoid this bias is to have a credible and efficient regulator, with sufficient enforcement power. This requires highly qualified, and independent, civil servants. *Finally*, the most important problem is that large fixed investments, which can not be re-deployed to other uses, are required. These investments are risky in countries with limited capital markets and unstable institutional environments. Although, as discussed earlier, Côte d'Ivoire has stronger institutions than many other developing countries, many observers believed that the risks were still too high to implement a full concession, especially since the contract includes systems in secondary centers.
"The main advantage of a *lease* is that it is more attractive to private operators, who might otherwise be reluctant to get involved in risky environments. If the contract is well designed (i.e., if there are adequate incentives to develop the water system and to perform efficiently), private operators might be able to significantly improve the management of the system. Adequate incentive schemes should base the operator's revenues on bills collected, and should provide the operator with motivation to reduce 'unaccounted for water' (UFW) and to extend the network. If the firm can capture part of the benefits of cost reduction, the contract might also encourage them to reduce costs. This is the solution adopted in Abidjan and it surely explains part of the success of the contract. However, there are also problems with lease contracts. *First*, since the

operator is not responsible for investment, the incentive to overuse physical assets is particularly high. *Second*, because firms are not responsible for, nor involved in, the management of the debt, there is a bias towards investment. This bias is aggravated by the affiliation that many large water companies have with construction companies (e.g., SAUR is a subsidiary of the construction group, Bouygues). *Third*, unless the contract is very specific, since the operator's income is based on bills collected, there is a strong incentive for the leasing company to develop the network only in the most profitable areas. If there are public health externalities or equity issues, leases might result in under-investment, especially in poor areas. Requiring the operator to charge the same price throughout the country or charge poor residents a lower 'social tariff' will magnify this risk. *Fourth*, for the reasons mentioned above, there is a risk that competition from bidding will be very limited, especially for contract renewals. Several factors alleviate the difficulties listed for both concession and lease contracts. *First*, since water systems rely on technologies that are well established, inputs are easily identifiable and costs are easier to assess. Therefore, a relatively competent regulator can estimate the validity of claims made by the operator more easily than in other infrastructure sectors. For example, in Côte d'Ivoire, the experienced engineers at BNEDT could determine whether the operator needed to change a pump and, based upon international prices, how much they should charge. *Second*, since there are very few operators on the international market for water supply services, and they are fierce competitors, there are strong reputation effects. If the operator wishes to expand, and to gain other contracts elsewhere, they would want to avoid problems with existing contracts."

Source: Ménard and Clarke (2000).

Table 1.4. **Privatisations in the Water Sector**

Country	Company	Year	Method (% sold)	Main strategic investor(s)	Comments
Burkina Faso	Office National de l'Eau (ONEA)	2001	Management contract	Vivendi	In partnership with Cabinet Mazars and Guerard, Vivendi was awarded a 5-year support and service contract (supported by World Bank financing). The contract covers the management of the customer service and finance activities with the assistance of a permanent team of 3 experts on site.
Central African Republic	Société Nationale d'Eaux (SNE)	1991	Lease (75)	SAUR	In 1995, a 15-year lease/concession contract was signed with SAUR. However, the contract is less a lease contract than an *affermage* contract since the former state-owned company was split into 2 entities: - SNE, a 100% public company that owns the assets, - SODECA, the private operating company (with SAUR as main shareholder).
Congo, Rep.	Société Nationale de Distribution d'Eau (SNDE)	2002	Lease	Biwater	In February 2002, the UK firm Biwater was awarded a leasing contract to operate SNDE distribution activity, beating competition from SAUR and Vivendi.
Côte d'Ivoire	Société de Distribution d'Eau de Côte d'Ivoire (SODECI)	1988	Lease (51)	SAUR	The privatisation of SODECI was the first privatisation in the water sector in Africa. "As early as 1959, before independence, an international tender was launched to select a private operator which would be responsible for the provision of municipal water services in Abidjan. The French company SAUR won the tender and subsequently a new company, SODECI, was formed with SAUR as main shareholder" (Kerf, 2000). In 1987, a re-organisation of Ivorian water provision was initiated by the government, leading to a new contract that appears to be a cross between a concession and a lease. Although no state holding company responsible for ownership of the assets was set up, this role was performed by the line ministry, which makes the contract very similar to an *affermage* contract.
Guinea	Entreprise Nationale de Distribution de l'Eau Guinéenne (DEG)	1989	Lease (51)	SAUR	In 1989, DEG was split into 2 entities: - SONEG, a 100% state-owned company responsible for owning sector assets and for planning and financing investment, - Société d'Exploitation des Eaux de Guinée (SEEG), a joint venture between SAUR and Vivendi (formerly Compagnie Générale des Eaux) in charge of operations and maintenance, as well as the replacement of small pipes. At the end of 1999, the contract had reached its 10-year term, and the government signed an interim 1-year lease contract which came into effect on 31 December 2000. However, efforts to negotiate a new 15-year lease contract broke down, and SEEG was re-nationalised.

Table 1.4. **Privatisations in the Water Sector** (cont'd)

Country	Company	Year	Method (% sold)	Main strategic investor(s)	Comments
Mozambique	Water services in 5 cities: Maputo, Beira, Quelimane, Nampula and Pemba	1999	Concession (70)	Consortium led by Aguas de Portugal	Aguas de Moçambique is a joint venture resulting from the merging of the water services of 5 cities. A 15-year water concession for Maputo and Motola, as well as a 5-year one for the other 3 cities, were awarded to the consortium in 1999, beating competition from Suez and Vivendi. Initially, 38.5% of Aguas de Moçambique was owned by SAUR, 31.5% by Aguas de Portugal and 30% by local investors. In 2002, however, SAUR withdrew from the contract, selling its shares to Aguas de Portugal, which became the company's major shareholder.
Senegal	Société Nationale des Eaux du Sénégal (SONES)	1996	Lease (51)	SAUR	Rather than a 10-year lease/concession contract, this is an *affermage* contract which led to the creation of two distinct entities: - SONES, a 100% state-owned company which, according to Kerf (2000), was to receive the difference between total consumer payments and SDE's remuneration and which would be responsible, *inter alia*, for owning sector assets, planning and financing investment (except for the replacements undertaken by SDE) and monitoring the activities of SDE; - Sénégalaise des Eaux (SDE), the operating company, with SAUR as main shareholder.
South Africa	Dolphin Coast	1999	Concession (58)	Siza Water (subsidiary of SAUR)	Dolphin Coast, with a 30-year concession to supply water and waste-water services, was awarded to Siza Water (a subsidiary of SAUR).
South Africa	Nelspruit	1999	Concession (40)	Biwater	30-year concession contract.
South Africa	Johannesburg Water	2001	Management contract	Ondeo/Northumbrian	5-year water management contract in Johannesburg, which covers the city's six municipal water and waste-water facilities and its 3 million inhabitants.
Uganda	Ugandan National Water and Sewerage Corporation (NWSC)	2002	Management contract	Ondeo (subsidiary of Suez)	In January 2002, Suez subsidiary Ondeo beat Vivendi to land a 2-year contract to manage and operate the water supply and sewerage services of the Kampala area, taking over from a German technical assistance team.

Source: Authors' calculations, based on various sources.

Table 1.5. Privatisations in Water and Power

Country	Company	Year	Method (% sold)	Main strategic investor(s)	Comments
Cape Verde	Electra	1999	Concession (51)	Portuguese consortium led by Aguas de Portugal	A 49% stake was sold to the Portuguese consortium with the signature of a 50-year concession contract.
Chad	Société Tchadienne d'Eau et d'Electricité (STEE)	2000	Management contract	Vivendi	In January 2000, Vivendi was awarded a 30-year contract to manage STEE, which is to be privatised by 2005 at the end of a transition stage during which the company should improve its financial and technical performance. In Phase 2, Vivendi will take a controlling interest in the utility with at least 51 per cent of the share capital.
Gabon	Société d'Energie et d'Eau du Gabon (SEEG)	1997	Concession (51)	Vivendi	Under the new ownership, SEEG, whose performance had been poor before the 1997 sale, has made a profit.
Gambia	Gambia Utility Corporation (GUC)	1992	Lease	Management Service Gambia (subsidiary of the French company SOGEA)	Management Service Gambia (MSG) was selected as the lessee through competitive bidding. It started operation and maintenance, including replacement of small pipes and formulating proposals for new investment. The contract, however, was less a lease than an *affermage* contract, since the government decided to set up a wholly state-owned holding company to take decisions on the planning and financing of infrastructure replacement and new investment and to monitor the activities of MSG. However, relations between the state holding company and MSG were very strained, and they deteriorated further after the 1994 military coup. In the end, the contract was unilaterally terminated by the government in February 1995 when MSG initiated an aggressive campaign to disconnect non-payers.
Mali	Energie du Mali (EDM)	2000	Concession (60)	Consortium led by SAUR	The joint venture between SAUR and IPS West Africa (a subsidiary of the Aga Khan Fund for Economic Development) was given a 20-year concession of 60% of Energie du Mali (EDM). SAUR has a 65% stake in the joint venture, while IPS has the remaining 35%. Previously, SAUR was part of a consortium operating at EDM under a management contract from 1994.
São Tomé & Príncipe	Empresa da Agua e Electricidade (EMAE)	1992	Management contract	Safège (subsidiary of Lyonnaise des Eaux–Dumez)	The management contract terminated in 1995. EMAE belongs to the group of nine public companies that the IMF has been trying to convince the São Tomé government to privatise since 2000.

Source: Authors' calculations, based on various sources.

Table 1.6. **Privatisations in the Power Sector**

Country	Company	Year	Method (% sold)	Main strategic investor(s)	Comments
Cameroon	Société Nationale d'Electricité (Sonel)	2001	Concession (51)	AES-Sirocco	A 20-year concession was awarded in July 2001 ensuring the monopoly of the generation, transport and distribution of electricity.
Côte d'Ivoire	Compagnie Ivoirienne d'Electricité (CIE)	1990	Concession (51)	SAUR/EDF	In 1990, a leasing agreement was signed with CIE providing it with a concession to manage generation, transmission and export of electricity for a 15-year period, renewable for two 3-year terms. Ownership of assets and responsibility for investment remained with EECI, the public enterprise which had been responsible for managing the sector, while the capital of the operating company CIE was divided as follows: SAUR, 33%; EDF, 18%; Ivorian state, 49%.
Guinea	Société Nationale d'Electricité (SNE)	1995	Lease (66)	EDF/SAUR/ Hydro-Québec International	The 10-year leasing contract is an *affermage* contract. In 1995, SNE was split into two entities: - ENELGUI, a wholly state-owned asset-owning company, - SOGEL, the private operating company. However, the contract broke down in 2002, leading to the re-nationalisation of SOGEL and to its merger with ENELGUI to form a new state-owned company: Electricité de Guinée (EDG).
Tanzania	Tanzania Electricity Supply Company (Tanesco)	2002	Management contract	NETGroup Solutions (South African engineering firm)	NETGroup Solutions will be paid a management fee of $2.6 million for its basic services for two years. The contract led to a huge scandal after the newspaper *The East African* revealed that the firm's Tanzanian partner was a company owned by President Benjamin Mkapa's brother-in-law. Since then, the government has rejected a parliamentary demand to reveal the details of Tanesco's management contract, explaining that the privatisation process would continue in secret.
Togo	Compagnie d'Energie Electrique du Togo (CEET)	2000	Concession	Elyo/Hydro-Québec	According to PSIRU, "Hydro-Québec International and Elyo won the tender to manage Togo's state electricity company, CEET. The group offered $31.7 million (CFA francs 21.74 billion) for the five-year renewable contract beating competition from two other French companies, Vivendi and SAUR. HQI and Elyo have committed to pay off CEET's debts of CFA francs 7.5 billion to the CEB electricity generator and will also pay CFA francs 350 million annually to an electricity regulator, which has yet to be set up.
Uganda	Uganda Electricity Generation Company (UEGC)	2002	Concession	Eskom Uganda Ltd (subsidiary of Eskom Enterprises South Africa)	Eskom Uganda Ltd has signed a $500 000 concession agreement with the government in 2002 to run the power generation business at the Kiira and Nalubale power stations in Jinja.
Zambia	Zambia Electricity Supply Company (ZESCO)	1999	Management contract	Elyo/Lysa, subsidiaries of the Suez/Lyonnaise group	The management contract has been granted to carry out a pilot project to enhance the financial position of ZESCO. This should prepare steps towards a hypothetical privatisation of the company

Source: Authors' calculations, based on various sources.

Notes

1. This average value is calculated by dividing the total sale value by the number of transactions, excluding liquidations, management contracts, restitutions, leases and concession contracts whenever their value is equal to 0. It should be noted, however, that this method of calculating the value per transaction, though more realistic, can have the drawback of overvaluing it.

2. Of these four SOEs earmarked for privatisation, 50 per cent of Telkom and 10 per cent each of Denel and Transnet had been privatised as of June 2003.

3. To date, only the gas companies of Guinea-Bissau and Cape Verde have been privatised, and two more are pending (Gaz de Côte d'Ivoire and Togogaz).

4. Based on the World Bank Africa Privatization Database classification.

Chapter 2

Have the Objectives of Privatisation Been Achieved?

As noted by Makalou (1999, 2001), countries have had three main motivations for undertaking privatisation programmes:

1. the short-term **fiscal benefits** brought by privatisation proceeds and reduction of the massive subsidies granted to often loss-making SOEs, together with an increased tax base as firms become profitable and the number of transactions increases over the longer term;

2. the **positive economic and social impact of competition**: competition should encourage corporate efficiency, entail lower prices and improve access to services formerly provided by the state;

3. the **development of financial markets** and the **broadening of local participation** in order to attract foreign direct investment and stimulate private-sector development.

There is, however, a fourth factor that has very often motivated privatisation programmes: the World Bank and IMF conditionality arrangements that make financial assistance depend on the execution of the privatisation programme. In Guinea, for instance, the government received $102.6 million for investment in the water sector because it concluded a lease agreement with the private sector in 1989 for management of the capital city's water supply. In late 1999, the government of Mozambique, with backing from the World Bank, signed a contract with the multinational water company Bouygues to provide water to seven cities in Mozambique, and the World Bank and other donors subsequently granted a $117 million loan for rehabilitation of water system infrastructure. These examples clearly show the strong correlation between privatisation and international aid.

Conversely, experience shows that reluctance to privatise can lead to sanctions on the part of donors. In November 2000, the World Bank warned Kenya that it would receive only part of a newly approved $72 million emergency energy loan if the government did not hold to its promise to privatise power generating and supply enterprises. In December 2002, the IMF representative in Lusaka announced that Zambia would not get the $1 billion in debt relief promised under the Highly Indebted Poor Countries (HIPC) initiative if the Zambia National Commercial Bank (ZNCB) was not privatised.

While such pressures are sometimes justified (IMF officials pushed for the privatisation of the ZNCB in order to re-allocate donors' and taxpayers' contributions towards the social sectors such as education and health, instead of subsidising the bank), they can increase the risk of dramatic failures. This has often occurred when time pressure led to the implementation of a poor regulatory framework. In some cases (e.g. in Zimbabwe), the process even started without the backing of a law on privatisation. In many other cases, the privatisation process started before the private sector had been tuned up to ensure a smooth transition. The lack of incentive to encourage private-sector participation and to limit the level of competition on the market exposed privatised firms to serious financial difficulties, leading many of them to bankruptcy. This risk was clearly stated in early April 2003 at a conference in Washington, DC, when the World Bank's Vice President for Poverty Reduction and Economic Management declared that countries could renegotiate their privatisation programmes. This declaration broke new ground, as rigid adherence to the privatisation programme used to be a firm requirement for access to HIPC funds. It might inaugurate a more realistic way of implementing privatisation programmes, taking into account the distinctive characteristics of each country, and it could offer an opportunity to harmonise donors' programmes, which are sometimes in conflict in terms of both time frame and objectives.

The following section reviews the existing literature and case studies with the aim of assessing the extent to which the main objectives mentioned above (fiscal benefits, efficiency gains, welfare improvement and the broadening of local participation) have been achieved. This will enable us to draw some conclusions and identify some aspects that are crucial to successful privatisation, but that have been largely neglected to date.

The Fiscal Impact

Privatisation has often been promoted by the IMF and other donors as a means of improving the fiscal balance both in the short run, through the sale revenues (direct effect), and in the longer run, thanks to the broadening of the tax base and the disposal of loss-making companies that drain the government budget (indirect effect).

Although the direct fiscal effect of privatisation is difficult to assess — because, as noted by Davis *et al.* (2000), the amounts of cash that actually accrue to the budget are highly uncertain — this effect in sub-Saharan Africa up to end 2000 was generally small, though it was unequally distributed across the countries in the region. To give a partial idea of the direct fiscal impact of privatisation, we computed, for each country, the annual ratio of gross privatisation proceeds to GDP (see Table 2.1). The ratios are virtually always less than 1 per cent, with an average value for all sub-Saharan Africa of 0.35 per cent. Only 12 countries achieved performances above this average regional value. The countries displaying the highest ratio are characterised by a relatively small GDP (less than $6.5 billion) and by major privatisation transactions, such as the sale of a 65 per cent stake in Cabo Verde Telecom in 1995-96 for an estimated $30 million, the privatisation of several units of Zambia Copper Mining in 1997-98 for a total value of more than $500 million and the listing of the Ashanti Goldfields Corporation in Ghana in 1994. Although no major transaction took place in Malawi, it shows a relatively high ratio compared to the other sub-Saharan countries, mainly because its average GDP was just over $1 billion for the 1990-2000 period.

The total privatisation proceeds to end 2002 are estimated at $8.8 billion, a very low figure compared to the developed countries. For example, privatisation proceeds in Italy alone totalled $108 billion over the 1985-2000 period (Mahboobi, 2002). Relative to GDP, Italy's privatisation proceeds fall to 0.6 per cent, still well above the sub-Saharan African average of 0.4 per cent. For purposes of comparison, it is worth mentioning that the average ratio of privatisation proceeds to GDP for the OECD area as a whole[1] over the 1985-2000 period is 0.5 per cent, with Japan, the best performer in terms of proceeds ($170 billion), exhibiting a proceeds/GDP ratio of 0.4 per cent. New Zealand, which ranks 18th in the OECD list in terms of privatisation proceeds and has a population of less than 4 million, enjoyed more privatisation revenue in this period ($11.5 billion) than the above 36 African countries combined, with a proceeds/GDP ratio of 1.5 per cent. The low overall figure for the value of proceeds in sub-Saharan Africa is all the more striking since, as Nellis (2003)

Table 2.1. **Privatisation Sale Values as Ratios of GDP and Government Revenue**
(percentages)

	Average annual sale value during active privatisation period, as % of average GDP, 1990-2000	Average annual sale values during active privatisation period, as % of average annual government revenue (ex. grants), 1990-2000
Angola	0.04	0.09
Benin	0.22	2.16
Burkina Faso	0.09	0.67
Burundi	0.18	1.12
Cameroon	0.20	1.29
Cape Verde	1.71	6.97
Central African Rep.	0.12	1.23
Chad	0.06	0.92
Republic of Congo	0.18	0.67
Côte d'Ivoire	0.37	1.73
Ethiopia	0.29	1.61
Gabon	0.13	0.48
Gambia	0.20	0.95
Ghana	1.44	7.73
Guinea	0.15	1.37
Guinea-Bissau	0.10	0.80
Kenya	0.25	0.93
Lesotho	0.37	0.92
Madagascar	0.04	0.31
Malawi	0.11	0.76
Mali	0.31	2.05
Mauritania	0.07	0.30
Mauritius	0.54	2.48
Mozambique	1.02	8.76*
Niger	0.00	0.04
Nigeria	0.06	0.17
Rwanda	0.02	0.20
São Tomé & Principe	0.47	2.71
Senegal	0.43	2.56
South Africa	0.12	0.42
Sudan	0.12	1.34
Tanzania	0.80	6.78
Togo	0.59	3.76
Uganda	0.38	4.41
Zambia	1.92	9.99*
Zimbabwe	0.16	0.55
Average sub-Saharan Africa	**0.36**	**2.20**

*   The relatively high ratio of privatisation proceeds to revenue (excluding grants) for Mozambique and Zambia is due to the fact that grants normally account for 20 to 30 per cent of revenues.

Source: Authors' calculations based on World Bank, *African Development Indicators 2002*.

points out, privatisation proceeds may be significantly overestimated in African countries, as buyers sometimes fail to make payment on transactions that are recorded as complete. The main reason for the low amount of proceeds is that many SOEs listed to be privatised are heavily indebted. Even in the case of liquidation, governments still have to assume full liability for this debt. In the context of a transfer of ownership, when private investors buy back the firm debt, the government often has to sell at a discount price.

The ratio of privatisation proceeds to GDP is certainly not the most appropriate indicator for assessing the fiscal impact of privatisation, however, as the figures for GDP dwarf the privatisation statistics and the resulting ratio does not take account of the size of the budget. The low significance of this ratio led Campbell and Bhatia (1998) to suggest taking instead the average annual sale value during the active period of privatisation as a percentage of average annual government revenue (excluding grants). The results reported in Table 2.1 show an average ratio for sub-Saharan Africa of 2.2 per cent, with 10 countries (of the 36 reported in the table) displaying figures above this aggregate average. This suggests that the direct fiscal effect of privatisation is substantial for about one-third of sub-Saharan countries. Moreover, the average proceeds/revenue ratio in sub-Saharan Africa is higher than in the OECD area, where it is about 1.6 per cent, with Portugal ranking first at 5 per cent, New Zealand second at 4.1 per cent and 18 OECD countries exhibiting ratios below the OECD average. Compared to other developing countries, however, the ratio for sub-Saharan Africa is low. In particular, the proceeds/revenue ratios for Latin America and the transition countries are 8.4 per cent and 5.5 per cent respectively for the 1990-2000 period (the respective proceeds/GDP ratios are 1.3 per cent and 1.9 per cent).

The fiscal gains from privatisation are more evident in the long-term perspective, focusing on subsidy savings (elimination of direct budget transfers that subsidise commercially unviable enterprises or compensate for politically motivated under-pricing of an enterprise's services or products) and the increase in tax revenue. According to the Privatisation Commission of Burkina Faso, government subsidies to SOEs in Burkina Faso dropped from $28 million (1.42 per cent of GDP) in 1991 to $2 million (0.08 per cent of GDP) in 1999 as a result of privatisation. This suggests that privatisation can allow governments to realise considerable savings. The broadening of the tax base can also lead to substantial tax revenues for the government, although it often takes time for newly privatised enterprises to become profitable. As of 1998, the tax revenues stemming from the privatisation of 16 enterprises (including two tax-exempt firms) already amounted to a promising $10 million (0.4 per cent of GDP), even though they were still showing low profitability at that time (Commission de Privatisation, 2000).

While potentially significant in the competitive sectors, the fiscal impact can be considerably delayed in the network utilities sector. This is mainly due to continued public involvement in a sector that, by its nature, requires large investment programmes. If not subsidised, these substantial investments would lead private investors to increase their prices in the short run, which is politically unacceptable in the context of poverty reduction strategies. In Guinea, for instance, government subsidies to the public water agency, the Entreprise Nationale de Distribution de l'Eau Guinéenne (DEG), remained substantial after a lease contract was signed with SAUR and Vivendi in 1989 (Ménard *et al.*, 2000). The reason was that although an immediate price increase was politically difficult, large investments were needed to extend the water distribution network. The World Bank therefore provided a loan to the operating company SONEG in order to avoid a sharp increase in rates. However, the loan was guaranteed by the Guinean government, making it a disguised government subsidy if SONEG failed to repay the loan (a distinct possibility, as the partnership between the government and SONEG was problematic and finally led to the withdrawal of SAUR and Vivendi in 2001).

In conclusion, although privatisation receipts amount to less than 0.4 per cent of GDP in the majority of countries, the indirect fiscal benefits remain potentially high. The fiscal benefits should, however, be balanced against the fact that privatisation can be socially damaging. Stopping subsidy flows to sensitive and strategic network utilities (water, energy, railroads and telecommunications) could affect poor households if it entailed a switch from under-pricing to "cost-covering" tariffs. Nevertheless, as argued by Birdsall and Nellis (2003), "tax-financed subsidies provided benefits primarily to the non-poor in the form of employment at wages above the market, or under-pricing for those with access". A study conducted by Kebede (2002) shows, for example, that in urban areas of Ethiopia in 1996 around 86 per cent of subsidies on kerosene were captured by the non-poor, since the consumption of kerosene increases with income. Furthermore, even when significant rates of subsidies are applied on the official market (in Ethiopia, kerosene and electricity subsidies were around 19 and 46 per cent of their respective prices in 1996), many poor people are forced to buy from secondary markets, and the benefits from low official prices are principally enjoyed by the rich. According to Kebede (2002), subsidies do not appear to be crucial to making energy accessible to the poor because the cost of accessing new energy resources, particularly that of electricity, entails up-front fixed costs that are generally not subsidised and that are affordable by the urban poor only if credit is extended to them or if these initial fixed costs are spread over the lifetime of the infrastructure concerned.

Efficiency Gains

Increased economic efficiency is one of the key objectives reiterated in most of donors' policy statements on their privatisation programmes. Privatisation aims to improve the performance of businesses by exposing them to a competitive environment and forcing them to earn high returns on investment and to organise production on an optimal basis. Adopting this objective has required a deep change of policy stance on the part of countries that had put their economic faith in government planning, control and intervention. Consequently, Andreasson (1998) argues that this radical change requires time and is still highly dependent on the nature and enforcement capacity of governments in place. In an earlier phase of privatisation in Tanzania, for instance, the ruling party Chama Cha Mapinduzi (CCM) did not list increased economic efficiency as one of its objectives; more recently, however, President Mkapa decided to enhance economic efficiency through the privatisation process, showing that the Tanzanian authorities have gradually accepted the necessity of divestiture for economic reasons. This example gives credit to the "learning curve" applied by Kayizzi-Mugerwa (2002) to the privatisation process in sub-Saharan Africa.

The same initial reserve was observed in French-speaking West African countries, where political power has remained in the hands of those who had previously pursued state intervention — a particularly widespread phenomenon in this region due to the persistence of an interventionist colonial legacy (Cogneau, 2002). In contrast, the advent of new regimes in Zambia and Uganda may have enabled these countries more readily to adopt privatisation policies aimed at increasing economic efficiency. This is clearly stated by the Zambia Privatisation Agency: "SOEs were characterised by under capitalisation, high indebtedness, over-staffing and inefficiency which contributed to their inability to make profits and effectively rendered most of them unsustainable business ventures. They were also a drain on limited government resources through subsidies and non-payment of taxes. Most of the SOEs had low productivity and could not compete internationally"[2]. When the Movement for Multi-Party Democracy (MMD) came to power, privatisation was included in its manifesto as a cornerstone of economic reform, and it was conducted more as a practical way to recapitalise SOEs and to let them operate efficiently and viably.

Privatisation also offers economic advantages in the case of natural monopolies, even though the economic literature initially promoted public ownership in these sectors. At first, public ownership of natural monopolies was justified as a solution to imperfect competition, incomplete information and incomplete contracts. Since then, however, several economists, including Sheshinski and López-Calva (1998), have observed that public ownership can lead to substantial efficiency losses, overcoming in many cases the gains obtained by resolving these market failures. The key question therefore shifts from ownership of the natural monopoly to how to regulate the activity of private investors on the market to prevent them from taking advantage of their dominant position. Many sub-Saharan countries still need to achieve substantial improvements in order to establish proper regulatory frameworks that give private firms the right incentives to improve efficiency without deterring innovation. In such cases, the expected benefits of privatisation in natural monopoly sectors do not actually appear, because of the lack of adequate regulatory and enforcement institutions which could prevent private investors from abusing their dominant position. Enhanced efficiency in the supply of services such as water, electricity, transport and telecommunications could have a key influence over the rest of the economy through improved production processes and reduced user costs, making privatisation of such infrastructure-intensive services a central issue for sub-Saharan countries.

The following sub-sections present some empirical evidence of the efficiency gains obtained through privatisation in sub-Saharan Africa.

Competitive Sectors

Only a few studies have examined the operating and financial performance of newly privatised firms in developing countries. In one such study, Boubakri and Cosset (1998) present 79 newly privatised firms located in 21 developing countries (of which only Nigeria is in sub-Saharan Africa) that had gone through full or partial privatisation during the 1980-92 period. On the basis of this sample, which is diversified both geographically and in terms of levels of development, they came to the conclusion that during the post-privatisation period, former state-owned and parastatal enterprises had increased their profitability, their operating efficiency, their capital expenditures and their output, although to a lesser degree in developing economies. To confirm the results found for the lowest-income countries, Boubakri and Cosset (2002) conducted another survey that focused on 16 firms privatised in the early 1990s in five low-income and lower-middle-income African countries (Ghana, Morocco, Nigeria, Senegal and Tunisia). On the basis

72

of a "before and after" analysis, they conclude that operating and financial performance has not significantly improved after privatisation in these countries, and they even find a slight decrease in sales efficiency (sales to total assets) as well as output. The efficiency of capital expenditure seems, however, to have increased substantially.

When one considers country case studies, however, their overall results seem to be more promising. Andreasson (1998) attempts to measure economic efficiency by assessing the change in productivity and in value added after privatisation in Tanzania. His results show that privatised companies in Tanzania more than doubled their productivity (defined as the number of units produced per worker) during the first year of privatisation, mainly because of better capacity utilisation and a decrease in the labour force. He therefore reports that the total value added of privatised companies increased by more than 400 per cent. Two other studies cited by Nellis (2003) report similar positive results for Tanzania (Temu and Due, 1998) and Ghana (Appiah-Kubi, 2001).

This does not mean, however, that privatisation has in all instances a positive economic impact, regardless of the firm and the performance indicator under consideration. As shown in Table 2.2, there can be significant discrepancies between firms, even when the overall effect is judged to be "positive".

The economic outcome of privatisation is difficult to appraise in the case of Burkina Faso, as it coincided with the devaluation of the CFA franc. Here, however, the devaluation problems that would bias statistics in local currency are limited by the use of the current exchange rate against the dollar. Table 2.2 displays wide disparities across firms. SBCP, SBMC and SOBCA saw their value added increase by 19 per cent, 157 per cent and 133 per cent respectively between 1992 and 1995. In the case of CIMAT and SN-CITEC, no data were available on the pre-privatisation phase, but these two companies posted spectacular performances in the post-privatisation phase (1995-97), with value added increasing by 390 per cent and 276 per cent respectively. In contrast, three of the eight companies in Table 2.2 recorded decreases over the same period: GMB (-56 per cent), SIFA (-50 per cent) and SONAPHARM (-52 per cent). Nevertheless, for six of the eight companies, the levels of value added in 1997 were much higher than those registered before privatisation, showing that, though delayed, the overall impact of privatisation on value added has been positive.

Table 2.2. **Financial Performance of 9 Enterprises in Burkina Faso Before (1992) and After (1995-97) Privatisation**

(thousands of current $)

	Investment			Turnover			Value added			Net profit		
	1992	1995	1997	1992	1995	1997	1992	1995	1997	1992	1995	1997
CIMAT	-	1 132.7	614	-	9 466.2	27 404.4	-	-1 770.2	5 133.4	-	1 619.8	644.9
GMB	-	1 453.4	548.8	24 660.6	19 144.9	19 228.3	4 873.1	2 135	2 339.4	-	589.4	588.3
SBCP	15.9	230.5	188.2	1 703.9	5 001.7	6 135	424.1	503.2	946.8	515	110.3	286.4
SBMC	75.7	92.2	1.7	757.3	858	4 320	223.4	573.3	430.5	-31.8	88.2	-106.3
SIFA	185.5	136.3	211	24 543.3	12 256.7	19 607.4	4 130.9	2 064.8	4 167.8	-371.1	613.4	1 921
SN-CITEC	-	1 810.2	3 370.2	-	4 600.8	18 494	-	1 415.3	5 322.1	568	-2 888.8	2 766.5
SOBCA	46.2	90.2	65.5	1 480.5	1 152.7	674	227.9	531.3	308.7	-	84.2	12
SONAPHARM	34.1	306.7	199	9 651.5	5 581.1	4 473.1	1 348	647.50	627.7	-817.9	96.2	-236.7

Source: Privatisation Agency of Burkina Faso.

Finally, the empirical evidence, although it masks wide variations in performance across firms and countries, and often relies on samples that are too small to allow firm conclusions, tends to show that, on average, efficiency objectives have been at least partially met in sub-Saharan Africa regarding privatisation in competitive sectors.

Natural Monopolies

The available empirical evidence regarding efficiency gains is less promising in the utilities sector, with the exception of telecommunications. While revenues and profits in this sector generally increase after privatisation (mainly owing to price increases following a switch to cost-covering strategies), productivity can remain quite low, notably in the power and water sectors.

In the **water** sector, the privatisation of DEG in Guinea was followed by generally satisfactory performance as regards revenues and profits. Total revenues increased quite substantially in real terms after the signature of the contract in 1989, from $8 million in 1990 to $20 million in 1996 (up 160 per cent). Profitability also improved following privatisation: whereas DEG was losing large amounts of money before reform, SEEG's operating profits started to increase from 1993 to reach $6.8 million in 1996.

Much less improvement is seen, however, when one considers productivity indicators such as "connections per employee" and "output per worker". Although the number of connections per employee showed an immediate increase upon the signing of the lease contract, this was due to the large reduction in the workforce that followed privatisation: before the reform, DEG employed about 504 workers, while after reform, the two spinoffs SEEG and SONEG had only 312 and 43 employees respectively. After the initial increase, connections per employee stabilised and even dropped between 1994 and 1996.

Output per worker showed a sharp increase just after privatisation (due again to the large reduction in the labour force) and thereafter continued to grow steadily, but this was due less to water sales, which increased relatively slowly following the reform, than to revenues from construction and other works related to the water sector. Total factor productivity increased by 325 per cent from 1987 to 1990, then slowly declined by 38 per cent from 1990 to 1996.

Finally, although the rate of bill collection from private consumers (which had been very low before reform) improved significantly after privatisation, it remained low compared to other privately operated systems. In 1989 and 1990, only 75 per cent of the amount billed to private consumers was actually collected (compared to 98 per cent in Abidjan, Côte d'Ivoire, as reported by Ménard and Clarke, 2001), and the collection rate fell under 50 per cent in 1991 and 1992 before recovering to 60 per cent in 1996. These fluctuations are mainly due to governance issues: although the government, under pressure from donors, paid its bill regularly during the first two years of the lease, its contribution fell to less than 50 per cent of the amount billed in 1991 and then to 10 per cent in 1993.

In the **power** sector, changes in operating efficiency do not seem to have been spectacular either. The privatisation of the Compagnie Ivoirienne d'Electricité (CIE), however, offers an enlightening success story. In 1990, a leasing agreement was signed between CIE and the EDF/SAUR consortium, which acquired a 51 per cent interest and a concession to manage generation, transmission and export of electricity for a 15-year period, renewable for two three-year terms. Ownership of assets and responsibility for investment were retained by the old public enterprise EECI, which had been responsible for managing the sector before reform. The results in terms of operating efficiency have been relatively minor, amounting to a reduction of about 0.3 per cent in losses in transmission, an improvement of about the same magnitude in the ratio of miscellaneous intermediate inputs to output, as well as in labour efficiency, and an improvement in the quality of ancillary services. According to Leroy *et al.* (2002), however, the modest scale of the gains can be attributed not to mismanagement, but rather to the fact that EECI had been a rather well-run SOE. In addition, the government retained not only the assets and debts, but also the responsibility for investment, leaving little room for manoeuvre to the private investor.

As Leroy *et al.* (2002) strongly emphasise, however, an indirect impact of privatisation ultimately led to huge efficiency gains. The privatisation of the electricity sector in Côte d'Ivoire has stimulated the emergence of independent power producers (IPPs) and thus increased competition in power generation activities. IPPs are electricity-generating companies (aimed at expanding future power capacity) that are not owned by the distribution company but sell their output to the electricity distribution organisations or directly to larger customers. They may be created by selling existing power stations to a new owner or by licensing a company to build and operate a new power station. IPP projects have been an important form of private-sector participation in

Table 2.3. **Major IPP Projects in Sub-Saharan Africa as of August 2000**

Country	Capacity/place	Year project signed	Companies
Côte d'Ivoire	210 MW at Vridi	1990	CIPREL (SAUR/EdF joint venture)
	210 MW (Scheme VII)	1994	SAUR/EdF
	288 MW at Azito (BOOT project)	1998	EdF/ABB
Ghana	110 MW at Takoradi Power Station	1997	CMS-VRA
	110 MW Takoradi II	1999	CMS-VRA
	220 MW near Tema	1998	KMR Power, EPDL and Marubeni
	80 MW Tema	1999	Union Fenosa
Kenya	74 MW Kipevu II, Mombasa	2000	Cinergy, IFC, CDC
Namibia	750 MW at Oranjemund (Kudu)	1996	National Power, Shell, Nampower and Eskom
Nigeria	548 MW (build and operate)	1999	Enron
	276 MW Southern Nigeria	2000	Siemens
Senegal	60 MW	1999	General Electric
	37 MW	1998	HQI
Tanzania	100 MW at Dar es Salaam (contract disputed and now under arbitration with World Bank)	1997	Independent Power, Tanwat: venture between Tanzanians and a Malaysian Company
	110 MW Songo-songo region	proposed	Consortium led by Ocelot (Canada)
Uganda	250-300 MW at Bujugali (30-year BOOT)	1999	Nile Independent Power (joint venture between AES and Ugandan firm, Madhivani
	200 MW at Karuma Falls	proposed	International) Joint venture between Sole Craft (Norway) and Packwatch Power (Uganda)
Zimbabwe	660 MW at Hwange	1996	YTL Power (Malaysia)
	1 400 MW at Gokwe North	1998	Consortium of National Power, ZESA and minor private investors

Source: Bayliss and Hall (2000).

Africa's power sector and have recently become the main source of new power generation in several African countries (Table 2.3). According to Karekezi and Kimani (2002), in countries such as Ghana, Namibia, Uganda and Zimbabwe the capacity of IPPs is greater than the installed state-owned capacity. IPP projects were initiated in Côte d'Ivoire in 1990 through a power project contracted out to CIPREL (another consortium led by SAUR and EDF), in conjunction with the lease agreement with CIE, and were shortly followed by other projects in Côte d'Ivoire and other sub-Saharan countries.

According to Leroy *et al.* (2002), the privatisation of CIE was the trigger for the introduction of IPPs, since it helped to establish the conditions for the development of this side activity. However, IPP projects are not necessarily related to privatisation and can be implemented independently in the context of a liberalisation strategy. This was done in Angola, where the government in March 2002 authorised the creation of a private power company, Hidrochicapa (55 per cent of which is held by the Russian firm Alrosa), alongside the public company Empresa Nacional de Energia (ENE). Hidrochicapa is in charge of the building of a hydro-electric dam intended to provide electrical power to the Catoca diamond mine and to the population of the Lunda Sul region, in the north-east of the country.

If the direct efficiency gains have been modest in water and power sectors, they seem far more evident in the **telecommunications** sector, where extensive reforms were carried out from the mid-1990s (Plane, 2001). These more spectacular efficiency results are mainly due to the fact that telecommunications has been increasingly subject to competition through GSM licences. In Côte d'Ivoire, for instance, the incumbent CI-Telecom was privatised in 1997, and then granted seven years of fixed-line exclusivity while "managed competition" was introduced in the cellular market and free competition in value-added services (VAS). By March 2001, three cellular operators and a number of VAS providers had entered the market, literally changing the landscape of Côte d'Ivoire's telecommunications sector and improving the sector's performance tremendously (Laffont and N'Guessan, 2002). The number of lines per employee rose by more than 50 per cent in less than two years after the reform, as a result of staffing cuts and an increase in the number of lines. Between January 1997 and December 1998, the number of lines jumped from 130 000 to 180 131, a rise of almost 40 per cent. Simultaneously, operating costs per line decreased sharply, from CFAF 528 422 ($745) in 1995 to CFAF 330 237 ($466) in 1997, and even to CFAF 286 136 ($403) in 1998, which represents an overall 47 per cent decrease between 1995 and

1998. The firm's financial results also improved considerably, with total turnover rising by 70 per cent over the 1995-98 period and net profit turning positive after 1994 and reaching $6 million in 1998. This financial performance can be attributed not to large price increases but to large efficiency gains, as connection costs dropped by more than 60 per cent between 1990 and 1999.

Similar outstanding results were observed after the privatisation of Sonatel in 1997 in Senegal. A subsidiary of France Télécom acquired 33.3 per cent of the capital, and this was followed by a public offering of 17 per cent of Sonatel on the Francophone regional stock exchange (the Bourse Régionale des Valeurs Mobilières, or BRVM) in Abidjan in 1998. Since then, Sonatel has performed exceptionally well (Azam *et al.*, 2002), with turnover in 1999 nearly twice the 1994-96 average, and an increase of over 50 per cent in value added. Meanwhile, Sonatel cut its prices and improved the quality of its services. In 2000, the company recorded an outstanding net profit of CFAF 42.5 billion ($60 million) as a result of the growth in activity combined with good cost management.

In Uganda, a consortium consisting of the International Telecommunications Union's investment fund, WorldTel, and a Deutsche Telekom subsidiary called Detecon was invited in 2000 to begin negotiations for the acquisition of 51 per cent of Uganda Telecom Limited (UTL), the state-owned telecommunications company, with the assistance of the International Finance Corporation. The consortium was the sole bidder in the international tender, offering a total of $23 million. This sale of shares was the final stage of a well-managed public restructuring programme, which included the establishment of an independent regulatory agency, the Uganda Communications Commission, and the initiation of liberalisation through the licensing of a second cellular operator, the South African company MTN. This successful preparation phase explains UTL's good financial results: in 1999, UTL made a net profit of $6.2 million, after a long period of deficits. Local and national long-distance service costs were cut drastically, from $0.20/mn to $0.05/mn and from $1.45/mn to $0.10/mn respectively over the 1989-2001 period.

The good results obtained in the telecom sector were mainly due to the introduction of competition through the awarding of GSM licences in conjunction with (or, as in Uganda, in preparation for) privatisation. As pointed out by Rosotto *et al.* (1999), "the introduction of new cellular players in the market, capable of offering new services and attracting new subscribers, tends to increase overall investments as well as revenues in telecommunications". This issue will be further analysed in the section on the welfare impact, where improvements in prices, access and coverage will be considered.

The Employment Issue

As privatised enterprises are not well monitored, accurate figures on pre- and post-privatisation employment levels are generally unavailable, making the debate highly ideological. Reliable data and sound analysis on the subject are greatly needed, as the most persistent and organised opposition to privatisation in Africa has come from organised labour. Privatisation programmes have led to many strikes during the last few years. In July 2002, thousands of Burkinabè workers went on strike and marched through the main streets of Ouagadougou to protest against the privatisation programme and the 5 200 job cuts the unions claimed it entailed. The fact is, however, that the sketchy evidence available is somewhat ambiguous as to the effect on employment, depending on the sector and the time horizon considered.

In the short run, privatisation tends to entail immediate redundancies because public enterprises are dramatically overstaffed, but this varies from sector to sector. In the nine enterprises in Burkina Faso's competitive sector that were privatised between 1992 and 1995, the overall number of employees increased by almost 20 per cent over the period. Table 2.4 shows, however, that this increase was entirely due to the dramatic increase in staff at CIMAT, SBMC and to a lesser extent SBCP, while the other businesses showed slight decreases in staffing.

Other statistical data show that of the 22 enterprises privatised in Burkina Faso up to 1999, the 16 sold through competitive sale of shares recorded an overall net increase of 135 jobs. The 1 047 redundancies reported during the privatisation process as of end 1999 came from four liquidations, and the affected workers were already technically unemployed due to the suspension of activity of these firms.

The above empirical evidence thus tends to show that, at least in the competitive sector, privatisation in Burkina Faso did not have the catastrophic impact on employment denounced by the unions.

According to the World Bank, the case of Zambia is more ambiguous. Originally hailed as a success story, it was subsequently described as much more problematic in terms of employment impact (Nellis, 2003). Although the privatisation of some 280 firms by the Zambia Privatisation Agency did not lead to many liquidations, it did lead to substantial lay-offs, especially in the copper mining sector, with great impact on the local economy. However, the privatisations also helped create new jobs through the development of private initiatives, making it difficult to assess the overall employment balance.

Table 2.4. **Number of Employees Before and After Privatisation**

Name	Number of employees	
	Before	After
CIMAT	11	169
GMB	156	126
SBCP	41	58
SBMC	62	170
SIFA	200	160
SN-CITEC	342	307
SOBCA	49	40
SONAPHARM	52	48
Total	**913**	**1 078**

Source: Privatisation Agency of Burkina Faso.

More generally, many studies indicate that, after registering a sometimes significant decrease the year after privatisation, employment in competitive sectors generally stabilises and then climbs to levels higher than those before privatisation. Andreasson (1998), for instance, provides clear evidence of this upward trend in Mozambique and Tanzania, occurring only a couple of years after the privatisation phase.

It is more challenging to assess the effect of privatisation on employment in the utilities sector, where the monopoly status of firms has generally led to inordinately high levels of overstaffing. The International Labour Office (1998) points to the major workforce reductions, as much as 50 per cent in some cases, that have followed privatisation in the water, electricity and gas sectors. Reduction of staffing levels is seen as an imperative (at least initially) in order to cut costs and boost productivity, since considerable overstaffing and insufficient ongoing training to keep staff up to date with changing technology and methods of work organisation are serious obstacles to efficiency. The ILO (1998) study shows that these heavy cuts were not followed by new recruitment in the longer run.

That said, the employment impact varies depending on the utility considered. According to the ILO (1998), redundancies in the water industry have usually been less severe than in electricity, since in many cases water supply has remained under strong public control. For instance, privatisation of water in Guinea through a lease contract in 1989 left employment levels virtually unchanged (from 506 in 1988 to 503 in 1996). In the power sector, however, jobs have been cut on a larger scale. The privatisation of electricity in Côte d'Ivoire through a 15-year concession contract signed in 1990 led to a gradual decrease in employment from 3 930 to 3 068 in 1995, a 22 per cent reduction. The restructuring of Eskom, a large public enterprise involved in the generation, distribution and sale of electricity in South Africa, resulted in a 40 per cent reduction of the workforce, from 65 000 to 39 000 over the 1992-98 period, as a way of preparing for privatisation.

Justified though the redundancies may be, the statistics on job cuts provided by labour unions have led the African national authorities to become more attentive to preserving jobs during the privatisation process so as to increase the acceptance of privatisation among the population. Gupta *et al.* (1999) point out that when a state-owned enterprise is offered to private bidders, retention of existing staff is more and more often either an explicit criterion or a major consideration in the selection process. In Burkina Faso, Société Sucrière de la Comoé (SOSUCO), whose privatisation in 1998 is considered a success story, was sold to the bidder that submitted the lowest of the four bids in competition but also pledged to maintain the entire labour force and to make substantial new investments. This choice did not prevent SOSUCO from posting an outstanding financial performance the following year.

As a further cushion against the negative social impact of job redundancies, social safety nets are negotiated between governments, companies and trade unions before privatisation. In some cases, they include severance pay for workers made redundant, dismissal with compensation, early retirement schemes, training, retraining and redeployment. Eskom, faced with the prospect of the sale of a 30 per cent share to the private sector by end 2003, is offering four different packages in order to soften the impact of restructuring. The most generous one is a voluntary separation package available to employees when the restructuring of a unit of the company is imminent. Such packages have in some cases a considerable impact on workers' income. For example, Bayliss (2002) points to the case of public-sector employees who have not been paid for long periods of time, and see such packages as "transitory income sources".

In some countries, governments even combine severance packages with business retraining and redeployment support (counselling, job search assistance, small business support) to help laid-off workers re-enter the labour market or become self-employed. In the utilities sector, one way to redeploy redundant workers is to help them set up co-operatives or small businesses as subcontracters for the newly privatised company, handling activities previously conducted by the state entity (for some types of jobs, service contracting improves performance incentives). In Guinea, the privatised water management company SEEG helped its approximately 250 laid-off workers to establish co-operatives to provide services such as new connections, canal maintenance and landscaping. Overall, about 20 small enterprises were founded, all of which are subcontracting for SEEG (Kikeri, 1999).

With respect to the workforce that remains after the reform, privatisation can lead to a re-allocation of the former wage bill in a proper, possibly more progressive way and to improvements in labour practices. In Côte d'Ivoire, the partial privatisation of CIE is considered by Leroy *et al.* (2002) to have led to higher wages overall and a net appreciation of the 5 per cent of the share capital allocated to employees at the time of privatisation. Similarly, in a survey covering eight firms in Benin in 1996, the World Bank noticed better working conditions and increased training opportunities in the post-privatisation phase. In the car servicing company SONAEC, for instance, training programmes in automotive engineering and maintenance were introduced, while Société Béninoise de Textiles established a flexible workday schedule and employee-of-the-month bonus scheme (Campbell and Bhatia, 1998).

The Welfare Impact: A Crucial Issue for Privatisation in the Utilities Sector

In the context of poverty reduction strategies, assessments of the outcome of privatisation in Africa cannot be limited to fiscal benefits and gains from the business perspective. The impact of privatisation must also be considered from the perspective of consumers and the general well-being of the population, especially when assessing transactions in the strategic utilities sector. Assessing the overall impact of privatisation in the network utilities sector is difficult, however, since, as noticed by Ayogu (2001), network utilities provide services that are part of the consumption basket of all residents and also serve as inputs in production. The privatisation of utilities therefore affects all actors — the private sector, government and the population — who obviously have different interests.

In order to grasp the conflicting interests at stake, Ménard and Shirley (1999) distinguish between groups likely to "win" and groups likely to "lose" following water-sector reforms. Among the potential winners, Ménard and Shirley first mention the segment of the population that initially has no access or rationed access to water, or receives poor quality of service. For instance, in 1990, the privatisation of the water sector in Conakry was strongly supported by the urban population, which suffered from great deficiencies in water provision (in terms of both quality and access). The private investors likely to take over the newly privatised company constitute a second potential group of winners, as long as their property rights are preserved. Lastly, politicians can benefit from increased tax revenues and the reallocation of these funds towards measures advocated by their constituents.

Ménard and Shirley (1999) also define three groups of potential losers. The first consists of people either illegally connected to the network or benefiting from discounted tariffs prior to the reform (generally registered as "unaccounted for water", or UFW) who are forced to pay their bills once the metering and billing systems are enforced or improved. A second potential group of losers is made up of bureaucrats and politicians who benefit from the existing system; in Guinea, for instance, politicians and high-ranking civil servants had almost free access to water and could use water connections to gain support from their clienteles. Finally, a third segment of the population that traditionally resists reform is salaried employees, and especially trade unions, which oppose the redundancies that follow privatisation. In the long term, job cuts are generally followed by the creation of new jobs, although, as mentioned above, these new jobs sometimes involve different categories of personnel not necessarily affiliated with the same unions. As the following sections will show, however, potential winners (lower-income domestic users in particular) can paradoxically become the actual losers of the reform if the regulatory framework and enforcement capacity are very weak, as the expected improvements in tariffs and access may not materialise.

As a result of these diverging interests, privatisation in network utilities is highly controversial. Polemics around privatisation of the water sector, unanimously considered the most "strategic" public good in developing countries, appear to be particularly revealing of the special status of utilities. According to Mookherjee and McKenzie (2002), the privatisation of utilities is typically a source of public discontent. These authors analyse the distributive impact of privatisation in Latin America and find rather positive outcomes that are not consistent with the commonly observed popular disenchantment with privatisation. The reasons for this "perception gap" are discussed in Box 6.

Box 6. **Sources of Public Misperception Regarding Privatisation in Utilities: The Case of Latin America**

"The divergence between popular opinion and the results of the studies reported here could also stem from biases in the process by which popular perceptions are formed, as well as the implicit use of different standards of fairness than are customarily applied by economists. Among the many possible sources of bias, lack of adequate information is probably the most important. Popular views are shaped by extreme cases that invite media attention, while widely diffused benefits are rarely noticed. Many of the benefits accrue to a wide range of customers, each of whom may be benefiting moderately; their improved welfare is overshadowed, however, by the dramatic losses of a few workers or customers.... This type of bias reflects the tension between statistical evaluation of economic outcomes and the way that mainstream views emerge on public policy issues, which Tom Schelling eloquently describes as the tension between personal and statistical lives (or, in this case, between a few personal tragedies and the widespread statistical benefits calculated by aggregating the fortunes of diverse individuals within any given income or expenditure class).

Psychological biases also tend to pervade popular opinions. First, the psychological phenomenon of loss aversion causes individuals to react more sharply to losses relative to the status quo than they do to gains. They tend to focus on the immediate short-term implications (such as job layoffs) without following through to the intermediate term (when the laid-off workers may be rehired). Second, privatisation is commonly lumped together in the popular perception with other promarket reforms, such as fiscal contraction and trade liberalisation that collectively constitute the Washington consensus. Separating out the distinct roles of these different elements of policy reforms is a forbidding exercise for academic experts, let alone the common citizen. It is also difficult to isolate the effect of privatisation from the effects of macroeconomic shocks or other technological changes occurring in the economy, of which there were many throughout the 1990s. Such negative associations may cause citizens to overlook the benefits of privatisation. Finally, there is a tension between some deeply held ideological principles (for example, that basic needs, such as water or electricity, should not be subject to the profit calculus of multinational corporations) and the reality of how state-owned enterprises actually perform with regard to the fulfillment of these basic needs. The fact that popular discontent is most severe in the case of water privatisation lends credence to this view. Suspicions that shares in public enterprises were given away to cronies of political elites or that the proceeds from privatisation have not been used in the public interest probably fuelled the discontent. Finally, there is a widespread pessimism concerning the ability of market pressure, the media, and regulatory oversight to constrain private enterprises to meet the public interest, which, though realistic in some instances, is exaggerated in many others."

Source: Mookherjee and McKenzie, 2002.

Impact on Tariffs, Access and Quality/Reliability

According to Birdsall and Nellis (2002), the privatisation process may have profitable distributional impacts on a long-term basis that can create more equitable pricing and delivery conditions. The short-term impact of privatisation, however, can vary widely depending on the sector under study, as is demonstrated in the following sub-sections.

Impact on Tariffs

The evidence shows that privatisation can affect prices in two different ways. On the one hand, prices may be pushed downwards by the increased competition that often accompanies the change of ownership. This is usually the case in the telecommunications sector, with the granting of one (or two) mobile licences as well as in some cases a second fixed-line licence, and the downward pressure can be strengthened by an increase in efficiency. On the other hand, in many cases prices rise after privatisation, especially in the power and water sectors. Such increases are often justified by the fact that governments generally set prices below cost-covering levels, making a re-adjustment necessary after privatisation if the activity is to become profitable.

In the case of network utilities, however, there is no need for price increases to finance the upgrading, maintenance and extension of infrastructure because of the kinds of privatisation contracts used. As we have seen, the private investor is generally responsible only for the operating activities, not the huge investments required for the construction of infrastructure, which remains under state ownership and control. In this case, price increases are not justified since the costs of investment are covered by the government.

In order to prevent the private investor from capturing a monopoly rent, regulation policies mainly focus on tight regulation of prices. These policies often consist in setting a "price cap" prior to privatisation that is deemed likely to create proper incentives for private investors both to reduce costs and to extend the consumer base through improved quality and hence increased demand for connections. The price cap is often determined in such a way as to cover operating costs and appears to be most effective when introduced by the government and regulatory authorities before privatisation. In Zimbabwe, for instance, when planning to reform the Zimbabwe Electricity Supply Authority (ZESA) in early 2000, the government clearly mentioned the need for tariff increases in the draft white paper: "There is need for accelerated tariff increases. Tariff increases are expected to contribute towards ZESA's financial viability, which has to be established before the reform process can begin." Once the price cap is properly set, it must be enforced by government and renegotiated only on an appropriate and rational basis, for example to take account of inflation.

Lastly, "cost recovery" does not necessarily entail price increases, but can also be achieved through better cost management. This happened in Côte d'Ivoire in preparation for the privatisation of CI-Telecom. In December 1990, the Comité de Privatisation was created to establish a strategic approach to the privatisation of telecommunications, including among its objectives the setting of fair and competitive prices. While local, long-distance and international tariffs stagnated between 1990 and 1997, when CI-Telecom was actually privatised, connection costs dropped over the period from CFAF 98 100 ($360) to CFAF 46 700 ($65)[3].

Other ways for privatised companies to increase revenues without relying only on price rises include seeking to reduce illegal connections and enlarge the consumer base, with the long-term result of spreading the cost over a larger population and hence allowing price cuts.

Price increases are thus not systematic. Whether they are implemented depends on the commitment of the political leadership and on the specific characteristics of the sector under consideration. In telecommunications, the keen competition introduced by mobile telephony has led to price cuts. In sectors less open to competition, regulation plays an important role in price setting.

Telecommunications

Price increases have been rare in telecommunications, since privatisation in this sector has often been accompanied by the introduction of competition, which tends to offset tariff increases in formerly subsidised local fixed-line telephony. This ultimately enables "tariff rebalancing" to make international service prices more affordable.

In Côte d'Ivoire, the decrease in connection costs initiated in 1990 was sustained after the privatisation of CI-Telecom in 1997, with a drop from CFAF 46 700 in 1997 to CFAF 38 900 in 1999. This was achieved through the introduction of competition. Before 1997, the public operator was the only provider on the market, whereas from 1997 to 2001 it was joined by 18 competitors (three mobile operators, two voice-mail operators, three call-box operators, ten Internet service providers).

In Senegal, the privatisation of Sonatel in 1997 was followed by price cuts. Connection fees dropped by 50 per cent in July 1998, from CFAF 87 700 to CFAF 43 900 for ordinary lines. The cost of calls between two *départements* in the same administrative region was reduced from CFAF 133 per minute to CFAF 50. The price of international calls was cut five times between February 1998 and June 2000, by 10 per cent, 15.5 per cent, 10 per cent, 8 per cent and 25 per cent. These cuts made Senegal's international call tariffs lower than those of the neighbouring countries. In 2000, the cost of calling Senegal from Mali and Côte d'Ivoire was respectively CFAF 700 and CFAF 535 per minute, while the reverse call cost only CFAF 283. The cost of calling France from Senegal was less than half that of calling France from Côte d'Ivoire, while calling the USA was three times cheaper. This good performance was mainly due to the introduction of competition, which coincided with the Senegalese government's awarding of a second GSM licence to Sentel (a subsidiary of the US company Millicom International) in July 1998. Revealingly, the price decreases started in July 1998 and ended in 2000 when Sentel's operating licence was withdrawn by the second government of Abdoulaye Wade, seven months after his election in March. This interesting episode reflects not simply a change of government but a change in the valuation of the private operator's performance, which led President Wade to reject the privatisation policy of the former socialist coalition. The contract was terminated because of what was perceived as the private investor's insufficient adherence to its engagements, which reveals the new government's mistrust of the regulatory framework set up by its predecessors. The Senegalese case shows how necessary it is to have a strong regulatory framework, in order to avoid misperception and misinterpretation as much as possible.

Competition is thus not necessarily a sufficient condition for successful privatisation (defined as tariff reductions together with greater access) in the telecom sector. A strong regulatory framework and political commitment are needed before the sector is opened up to competition. Further demonstrations of this are given in the sub-section on the access and quality impact of privatisation, especially with respect to the power and water sectors.

Power and Water

In contrast to telecommunications, privatisation in the power and water sectors has shown disappointing results in terms of price cuts, owing to the difficulty of opening these sectors up to competition. Their "natural monopoly" status makes it more difficult to design privatisation contracts that set the right price incentives. Failed privatisation operations in these sectors have led international donors to believe that any attempt at privatising should be preceded by the establishment of a strong regulatory and enforcement system, by deep restructuring and reforms in the way these systems are managed, and in particular by increases in tariffs to cost-covering levels.

Power

The pending privatisation of Uganda's power company provides a good illustration of this change in approach. In January 2002, both the Indian firm Tata Power and the US company Cinergy Global Power, the two pre-qualified bidders for the 20-year concession of the generation and distribution arms (Uganda Electricity Generation Company, or UEGC, and Uganda Electricity Distribution Company, or UEDC) of the former electricity parastatal, decided to withdraw as a consequence of a reduction in power tariffs imposed by the parliament. This event led the government (with the backing of the World Bank, which had long been pushing for price reduction) to adopt a new privatisation strategy based on the restructuring of the SOE, mainly through tariff increases likely to ensure its viability and to create greater incentives for potential investors. A tariff increase was adopted in May 2002. As a counterpart to this effort, the new investors in UEDC were required to invest at least $70 million over five years to strengthen the existing distribution system — regarded as the main capacity constraint at the time — and to extend the grid. This pragmatic way of preparing for privatisation bore fruit when, in late August 2002, Eskom Uganda, a subsidiary of Eskom Enterprises of South Africa, offered $38.5 million for UEGC.

Such tariff increases are not popular and may in some countries lead to riots and political debate, as in the cases of Ghana and Uganda. In Kenya, many industrialists claimed they had been forced to close and redeploy to other industries following the price increase. The central issue, however, becomes the extent to which privatisations in the power sector and the subsequent tariff increases are detrimental to poor consumers. While it is generally believed that electricity price hikes are detrimental to them, empirical studies (Kerekezi and Kimani, 2002) show that poor are adversely affected by such hikes only if the country's electricity coverage is relatively high, implying that both poor and non-poor are users. In the case of Uganda, where only 5 per cent of the population has access to electricity, only the extremely rich are connected to the grid, and hence subsidies cannot be justified on equity grounds. The situation changes in countries where coverage levels are high. In South Africa, for instance, 70 per cent of households have access to electricity, which means that about half of the poor are connected to the grid. In this case, Karekezi and Kimani(2002) shows that price increases and the removal of subsidies strongly affect the poor. Overall, most African countries exhibit low levels of electrification, which implies that tariff increases and the removal of subsidies will have only a weak impact on the poor. Consequently, attempts to "underprice" service in the power sector are not defensible on grounds of equity, in stark contrast to the water sector, where "universal service" (and thus "social tariffs") is absolutely necessary. Moreover, revenues from wealthier users can be used to extend infrastructure to reach rural populations. Finally, tariff increases are generally accompanied by improvement in both access and quality of service (with fewer blackouts), which, though not necessarily perceived by consumers in the short run, can in fact largely compensate for price increases.

Water

Tariff increases in this sector have been less systematic owing to the absolute necessity of providing water service to as many households as possible. Price discrimination, in which the better-off are charged more for the service, has been a common way of accomplishing this. In the case of Gabon, the awarding of a concession contract in 1997 to Veolia (alias Vivendi Water) for the management of the multi-utilities company Société d'Energie et d'Eau du Gabon (SEEG) led to lower prices for both electricity and water service.

The overall variation in prices mainly depends, however, on the type of price regulation used and on the degree of information asymmetry. The price regulation systems most often used are cost-plus regulation and price caps. Cost-plus (also called "rate of return") regulation has been widely used as a way of ensuring fair treatment for both the firm and the consumer. It consists in setting prices on the basis of costs, as disclosed by the firm, adding a specific mark-up in order to ensure a profit to the firm, while protecting consumers from arbitrary tariff increases. Experience has shown, however, that such price regulation is very difficult to implement, as the firm has no incentive to reduce its costs and every temptation to overestimate them. The reason why it has been so widely used relates to the desire of governments to attract private investors. However, such price regulation has generally led to large price increases. In the case of Guinea, cost-plus regulation was misapplied owing to the inability of SONEG, the regulator of the lease contract, properly to verify the actual costs of the operating company SEEG, and the resulting price increases were excessive. Before privatisation, in 1988, the price per cubic metre was the lowest in the region at $0.10/cu.m (compared to $0.45/cu.m in Benin and Togo, $0.85/cu.m in Côte d'Ivoire and $1.25/cu.m in Senegal at the same period), whereas the tariffs were increased in 1989 to about $0.25/cu.m so as to cover all of SEEG's and SONEG's local currency costs (i.e. staff wages). Owing to the cost-plus regulation, prices had increased by more than had been originally planned, and by 1996 had reached levels one-third higher than the initial targets.

Badly managed price regulation stems mainly from information asymmetry, which can be dampened through auctioning and more precisely through concession/lease bidding. These methods allow governments to identify the actual operating costs of bidders and therefore to select the private company that delivers the service at the lowest price. Auctioning is becoming more and more frequent in sub-Saharan Africa in the privatisation of water systems. In Côte d'Ivoire, for instance, where prices are regulated on a cost-plus basis, a renewal of the water lease contract in 1988 involved the use of a "bidding threat". SODECI was threatened with having to face other bidders if it did not revise its tariffs. This led to a very substantial reduction in real prices both for domestic users (-20 per cent) and for industrial users (-23 per cent), and forced SODECI to abide by a stronger tariff discipline, which helped to dampen the effect of the CFA franc devaluation in 1993. Overall, in 1997, the average price of water was $0.54/cu.m compared to a pre-reform average price of $0.85/cu.m.

An auction is only "fair", however, when there are enough bidders, which, as noted above in the section on privatisation methods, is not always the case. In Cameroon, for instance, there was only one bidder (Ondeo) for the water supply concession in 2000. This shows once again the need to restructure companies before they are privatised so as to ensure their financial viability. Moreover, combating information asymmetry is not always an easy task, even when the needed political will exists. For instance, the 1988 reform in Côte d'Ivoire stipulated that SODECI had to assume more responsibility for investment, since SODECI, though responsible for the planning and execution of investment, bore none of the financial risk. It was thus decided that, for investments costing more than CFAF 120 million (about $220 000 in 1996), competitive bidding should be organised. SODECI got round this rule, however, by splitting major investments into small ones that could be implemented without a tender, which explains why no large investments were undertaken during the decade following 1988.

Information asymmetry related to cost-plus regulation can be offset by using a second price regulation method: the price cap system. This consists in protecting consumers by limiting the price that a firm with market power can charge. At the same time, it provides incentives for the firm to become ever more competitive. This system has not been widely used in sub-Saharan Africa. Although it creates greater incentives than cost-plus regulation and is more appropriate in countries with weak enforcement capability, the price cap system may lead the firm to focus only on the most profitable areas (in general, urban areas). Thus, even with price cap regulation, a strong regulatory framework with enforcement capability (specifying for instance the number of new rural connections to be operated by the private investor) is still badly needed.

Water privatisation also affects prices through improvements in metering, billing and collection, which are liable to reduce the amount of "unaccounted for water" (UFW). Although difficult to assess, amounts of UFW were usually incredibly high before privatisation but thereafter dropped to low levels by international standards (below 20 per cent). Not all countries enjoyed the same success, however. Whereas in Côte d'Ivoire SODECI, the firm responsible for maintenance, managed to achieve a 98 per cent collection rate, in Guinea the division of responsibility for maintenance between the public (SONEG) and private (SEEG) entities led to confusion and conflicts over the delineation of roles and to a dramatic drop in the collection rate from 75 per cent in 1989 to under 50 per cent in 1992. Such situations are highly characteristic of water privatisation implemented without sufficient political will. Despite SEEG's efforts to cut off water to customers who did not pay their bills and to put an end to the discounts and privileges accruing to civil servants, the collection rate did not improve. When donor pressure relaxed in 1991, the government stopped paying its bill, leading to a spectacular decrease in the collection of government fees, which dropped to 10 per cent of the amount billed in 1993.

The improvement in water bill collection that usually follows privatisation has led opponents of water privatisation to claim that the only objective of private investors was to bill water consumption without making any efforts to improve prices, coverage and quality. As we will see in the next sub-section, improvements in coverage and quality are real but highly dependent on government's ability to enforce the contract. Where prices are concerned, when the political will to provide "universal service" and to protect the poorest households exists, it generally results in fairly progressive tariffs. In Côte d'Ivoire, for instance, in addition to the implementation of a two-part tariff, "social" connection fees and unit prices have been established, thanks to cross-subsidies from urban to rural areas, and from industrial to domestic customers. More precisely, access charges for small (and often low-income) consumers are subsidised, with no charge for connection pipes less than 15 mm in diameter for private non-commercial connections. In 1997, low-income customers paid an average charge 2.5 times lower than large customers for connection, installation of a meter and advance payments for future consumption. Unit prices to low-income customers are also subsidised, through price discrimination according to the amount consumed (making it possible to distinguish between small, medium-sized and large non-commercial consumers) and the type of consumer (non-commercial, "industrial" and "administrative", i.e. public) (see Table 2.5).

The political commitment of Ivorian government and regulatory authorities to ensuring progressive tariffs for lower-income customers has led not only to the establishment of a price discrimination scheme, but also to continual price decreases in real terms, with the most spectacular drop coming in the area of "social" tariffs. Here again, as in the case of the power sector, the establishment of a strong regulatory framework backed by the political commitment needed for contract enforcement has played a key role in the success of privatisation. This applies with even greater force when one considers the impact of privatisation on access and quality/reliability.

Table 2.5. **Water Prices in Côte d'Ivoire, 1983-99**

(CFA francs per cubic metre)

	1983	1984-Sept. 1987	Oct. 1987-Jan. 1994	Jan. 1994-May 1996	May 1996-1999	Percentage change in real terms, 1987-97
"Social" tariff	187	187	159	159	184	**-36.1**
"Domestic" tariff	261	261	209	230	286	**-25.7**
"Normal" tariff	300	330	307	368	464	**-16.5**
"Industrial" tariff	525	458	350	424	532	**-28.7**
"Administrative" tariff	261	261	261	311	390	**-17.5**

Source: Ménard et Clarke (2000).

Impact on Access and Quality/Reliability

The Power and Water Sectors

Impact on Access

Privatisation is said to broaden access to services through network expansion that the former public firm could not properly finance. The problem is that private owners, being profit maximisers, may decide instead to withdraw from markets that the former public owner had pledged to serve, and invest only in profitable activities where they expect to make a commercial return, especially when they enjoy a dominant market position, as is the case in the power and water sectors. This is particularly true of concession contracts, where the financial risk of investment is borne by the private owner. Under such conditions, whenever the return on investment is not assured, there is a risk that the private investor will withdraw from the investment project. For example, the British water firm Biwater withdrew in December 1999 from a proposed private water project in Zimbabwe because the beneficiaries could not afford to pay a tariff high enough to accommodate the profit margin the company was seeking (Bayliss, 2002). The Biwater country manager for Zimbabwe, Richard Whiting, summed up the sometimes conflicting objectives of private versus social goals as follows: "Investors need to be convinced that they will get reasonable returns... The issues we consider include who the end users are and whether they are able to afford the water tariffs... From a social point of view, these kind of projects are viable but unfortunately from a private sector point of view they are not."

As shown in the case studies, however, privatisation in the power and water sectors is often followed by increases in access, although mainly in urban areas. After the lease contract was signed in Guinea, the number of connections did increase in absolute terms, but at a much slower pace than anticipated, and coverage remained low, especially outside Conakry. By the end of 1997, following the Second Water Supply Project, there was a total of about 31 000 connections, including 25 000 connections in Conakry (population 1.7 million), compared to 180 000 connections in Abidjan (population 2.7 million) at the same period.

Certain policy instruments can help improve water and electricity coverage in rural areas, such as cross-subsidisation and the introduction of small-scale providers. Cross-subsidisation is the main tool used in the water sector for supporting rural expansion, since it treats consumers equally by

94

charging rural users the same price as urban consumers. According to Trémolet (2002), none of the secondary centres in Côte d'Ivoire would be profitable on its own, and water service could not be provided in such areas without the surpluses made in Abidjan. In 2001, Abidjan accounted for 48 per cent of connections, 65 per cent of sales revenue and only 52 per cent of production costs owing to the proximity of the water source. The reform of 1987, however, transferred responsibility for rural water outlets from SODECI to the Ivorian government, suggesting that cross-subsidies were not properly implemented by the private operators. SODECI estimated that maintaining and operating rural water outlets had cost it about 10 per cent of its revenues over the 1982-87 period, but it was primarily the poor quality of the service provided by SODECI in remote areas that determined international donors to relieve SODECI of this responsibility. A survey conducted by the Ivorian regulatory authorities in 1986 showed that only half of the 13 500 water outlets that they checked were functioning.

A second instrument that is apt to improve coverage after privatisation is the introduction of competition by allowing small-scale providers to compete with the main operator for contracts. There have already been several experiences of liberalisation in power generation, via the division of the former state-owned electricity producer into several competing companies, or via tenders aimed at attracting independent power producers. The latter option is highly likely to increase rural coverage, especially since it is increasingly used by government because it requires only modest restructuring compared to that entailed by a privatisation process. It should be noted, however, that although competition is appropriate in certain segments of the power sector, it is less easy to introduce in the water sector.

Finally, a proper and well-enforced regulatory framework can be key to the improvement of access, particularly when the privatised operator has monopoly power and, in the absence of regulation, would likely serve only the most profitable segments of the market (urban areas). Examples of this may be found in South Africa and Ghana, where autonomous electricity regulators have been successful in expanding electrification in their countries. In South Africa, electrification programmes promoted by the National Electricity Regulator targeting the urban poor and rural communities have raised the electrification level to 50 per cent in rural areas and 80 per cent in urban areas. In Ghana, the activity of the Public Utility Regulatory Commission has helped to raise the electrification level from 15 per cent ten years ago to about 45 per cent today.

Impact on Quality/Reliability

In the power and water sectors, the key to obtaining the desired improvement in quality is to establish the regulatory framework and contract enforcement needed to make the private operator abide by its commitments. These elements must be implemented on a realistic basis, however, which requires strong political commitment to the restructuring of the incumbent prior to privatisation (the failure of the privatisation of Sonel in Cameroon is very revealing). When such requirements are not met, the impact on quality can be almost nil, if not negative. This is particularly true of the power sector, where failure to meet these requirements can lead to recurrent brownouts. In the water sector, however, private operators usually have sufficient expertise in water and sewage treatment, which generally leads to better service quality. Galiani *et al.* (2002), one the very few econometric studies that consider the impact of water privatisation on quality, focuses on the privatisation of local water companies in Argentina, covering approximately 30 per cent of the country's municipalities. Studying the temporal and spatial variation in ownership of water provision generated by the privatisation process, the authors find that child mortality caused by "infectious and parasitic diseases" (which are typically related to poor water and sanitation provision) and "perinatal diseases" fell by 5 to 7 per cent on average in areas where water service was privatised. Moreover, the poorest segments of the population experienced the largest gains in terms of quality improvements, with a 24 per cent drop in child mortality. Robustness tests confirm that this effect is probably due to privatisation alone.

Where sub-Saharan Africa is concerned, empirical evidence suggests that privatisation has a positive impact on quality. In Guinea, for instance, there is a consensus that the quality of piped water improved significantly after reform, with chemical and bacteriological contamination rates complying with WHO norms. If the improved quality is to benefit all, however, "social tariffs" must be set so as to enable poor households to continue to consume piped water. If such households are evicted from the market by high prices, the impact on the health of the population can be catastrophic no matter how great the improvement in quality. According to Bayliss (2002), this is what happened in South Africa, where an attempt to restructure the sector via a cost-covering policy led to a cholera outbreak that killed 260 people in Kwazulu Natal in August 2000. Residents in the area where cholera first appeared had previously enjoyed government-subsidised water provision, but under the cost-recovery policy were charged a registration fee of R51.

Telecommunications

Privatisation in the telecom sector has generally resulted in broader access. In Côte d'Ivoire, the privatisation of CI-Telecom improved fixed-line penetration per 100 people from 1.03 in 1997 to 1.80 in March 2001 (although the latter penetration rate is still insufficient), while mobile penetration grew at an exceptional rate from 0.26 to 4.46 per 100. However, the exclusive rights granted to the private investor have constituted a constraint on the achievement of greater gains in terms of access: although CI-Telecom has been granted exclusive rights until 2004 in the fixed-line sector in order to achieve the objectives set by the Ivorian government — such as extending coverage and improving quality of service without resorting to government subsidies or credit — the evidence shows that as of March 2001 the operator had not achieved the targets for rural telephony and service quality (whereas the targets for main lines and call boxes have been met). On the contrary, fixed-line penetration[4] increased instead in areas where the operator faced competition from mobile providers.

The fact that CI-Telecom performed better in terms of fixed-line penetration when facing the competition of mobile operators confirms the results of Wallsten (1999), in a paper that studies the combined effects of competition, privatisation and regulation on telecommunications performance in 31 African and Latin American countries (including 15 African countries, all in the sub-Saharan region except Morocco) from 1984 to 1997. Telecommunications performance is measured by main-line penetration, the number of pay phones per capita (which makes it possible to assess the extent of universal service), connection capacity (which the ITU defines as "the maximum number of main lines which can be connected"), the number of employees per main line (an indicator of labour efficiency) and the price of a three-minute call. Wallsten (1999) shows that competition (measured by the number of mobile operators in the country not owned by the incumbent) is positively correlated to main-line penetration, pay phones and connection capacity, but negatively correlated to the price of local calls. This is an interesting result, since privatisation alone (i.e. without competition) is negatively correlated to main-line penetration and connection capacity. Wallsten's result thus indicates that the introduction of competition is a necessary component of privatisation. The positive effect of competition can be further enhanced by the introduction of an independent regulator, since privatisation combined with an independent regulator would substantially mitigate the negative effects on main-line penetration. This suggests that the key to success for greater access in the telecom sector is to combine privatisation with competition under an appropriate regulatory framework.

This was the case in Senegal, whose telecom privatisation is regarded as successful. Its success was due to the introduction of competition from 1998 to 2000 and to the very early establishment of a regulatory framework. As early as 1985, the Senegalese government undertook a thorough reform of the telecom sector, merging domestic and international telecommunications activity and separating it from the post office. Although Sonatel was given monopoly rights over telecommunications in Senegal, a list of objectives to be achieved (over a three-year period starting in 1996) was defined, with the emphasis on extension of the network and on quality of service. This restructuring allowed Sonatel to post record-breaking performance, going well beyond the initial requirements, which in turn allowed the government to implement its privatisation smoothly, beginning in February 1995 when the privatisation act was passed by the National Assembly and ending in 1997 with the effective privatisation of Sonatel.

In the cases of both CI-Telecom and Sonatel, quality was improved as well, although quality indicators still do not meet the international standards of the ITU. For instance, prior to privatisation CI-Telecom had one of the highest failure rates in the Western Africa region (88 per cent in 1994 and 75 per cent in 1995, whereas the required ITU standard is 30 per cent), due to the poor state of the telecommunications network. One year after privatisation, failure rates for local, long-distance and international calls, though improved, still exceeded the ITU norm. However, CI-Telecom's efforts to improve quality seem to have brought results, and at least have been perceived by the population. According to a survey conducted by the Telecommunications Agency of Côte d'Ivoire (ATCI), 83 per cent of CI-Telecom customers believed that the quality of service had improved following privatisation, whereas 75 per cent noticed improvement in customer service. In Senegal, the success rate for local calls rose from 50 per cent in 1996 to 64.79 per cent in 1999 (close to the ITU norm of 70 per cent).

By contrast, where the regulatory framework is very weak, the situation can rapidly become untenable and the failure of privatisation blatant. In such a case, despite the presence of competition (whether in mobile or fixed-line telephony or both), private operators are under no pressure owing to the lack of a credible regulatory framework. This is what occurred in Ghana, where performance in terms of access and quality was very bad, despite the presence of an independent regulatory agency, the National Communication Authority (NCA). The NCA was established in 1996 by an act of Parliament (NCA Act 524), as part of Ghana's telecom sector reform policy initiated in the same year to introduce privatisation, liberalisation and controlled competition in the telecommunications industry. A few months later, in February 1997, Ghana Telecom was partially privatised through the sale of a 30 per cent interest to G-Com Ltd (a consortium of four companies, 85 per cent of which is owned by Telekom Malaysia) for \$38 million. The consortium was granted a five-year management contract under which the Ghanaian government, despite its 70 per cent majority stake in the company, left the management of Ghana Telecom to Telekom Malaysia. Such a privatisation scheme required a very strong regulatory framework so as to prevent Telekom Malaysia from using its market power to extract monopoly rents, but the interval between the creation of NCA and the partial privatisation of Ghana Telecom was too short for NCA to acquire sufficient regulatory know-how. Even the government seemed unwilling to make its voice heard: when its representatives on the board of directors resigned at the end of 2000, they were not replaced. Under such a poor regulatory structure, it is not surprising that Telekom Malaysia did not undertake the investment required by the contract it had signed with the government. Under the contract, Telekom Malaysia was supposed to provide a minimum of 400 000 additional fixed telephone lines, but when the management contract reached its term, the total number of fixed lines in the country was only 240 000 for a total population of around 20 million, and reliability was very low.

The lack of a regulatory framework was not counterbalanced by competition, even though competition was introduced very soon, in both the mobile and fixed-line markets, and is considered to be particularly intense. There are currently four competing mobile phone companies. In the fixed-line market, the government sought to create a duopoly by granting a Second National Operator (SNO) licence in 1997 to Westel (Western Telesystems), a joint venture between the US firm Western Wireless International and the Ghana National Petroleum Company. Once again, however, the lack of a regulatory framework soon proved fatal, since Westel had no incentive to adhere to its commitments. Whereas NCA was expecting Westel to install and operate at least 50 000 fixed telephone lines by the end of 2001, as of August of that year the fixed-line operator had installed only 2 636 lines and 166 pay phones, restricting its operations to the Accra and Tema metropolitan areas, where economic activity is concentrated. The press gradually realised that the privatisation was a failure as it became clear that the improvements in access and reliability expected by consumers would never come before the term of the management contract, and journalists subjected the operation to very sharp criticism throughout the year 2002 (see Box 7).

As in Senegal, where a new government had rejected those of its predecessor's accomplishments which it considered inadequate, the new political coalition New Patriotic Party (NPP) elected in Ghana in December 2000 decided to force the investors to abide by their commitment. The upshot was that the NCA decided in May 2002 to take legal action to compel Westel to pay the prescribed $1 500 penalty for each uninstalled line. The determination of the NPP government has already been thwarted to some extent, however. Alhassan (2003) reports that the attempt to make Westel pay a total amount of $70.5 million was impeded by the US assistant secretary of commerce for market access and compliance, who visited the country at that period and publicly condemned the Ghanaian government for its unfriendly attitude towards foreign investors, and in the end managed to have the Westel penalty reduced from $70.5 million to $28 million. As for Ghana Telecom, when the first five-year exclusivity period for fixed-line and international telephony was due for renewal, the NPP abrogated the original contract and signed a three-year management contract with Telecom Management Partner (TMP), a wholly owned subsidiary of the Norwegian telecommunications group Telenor ASA. Telekom Malaysia's loss of control over Ghana Telecom led the Malaysian company to offer to sell its 30 per cent stake back to the government, which should be done during the year.

The lesson to be drawn from Ghana's privatisation experience in the telecommunications sector is that countries engaging in privatisation reforms need time to get used to regulatory issues. This may be what led Ghana to establish a very good regulatory framework for the privatisation of the electricity generation company UEGC. This finding provides confirmation of Wallsten (1999) sequencing of regulation and privatisation in telecommunications reforms. Wallsten argues that establishing an independent regulatory authority prior to privatisation allows greater telecom investment, fixed-line penetration and cellular penetration than is possible in countries with no regulatory framework.

In both telecommunications and the power and water sectors, the regulatory framework and enforcement capacity have been shown to be crucial to improvements in access and quality. Although such a measure is not necessarily linked to privatisation programmes, the establishment of an autonomous regulatory body in the utilities sector allows radical improvements in access to services.

100

Box 7. **Scepticism of Ghana's Media towards Ghana Telecom's Performance in Terms of Access and Reliability**

Access

"Dark Clouds over Ghana Telecom", *Accra Mail*, May 2002

"An important lesson to be learned from the Malaysian Catastrophe is that any future contract with investors must have a yearly review concept. In the case of the Malaysian Catastrophe (which is really the fault of Ghanaians), the contract was signed for a five-year period with no yearly review. The investor's performance must be reviewed every year, according to specified targets, with the option of terminating the contract should their services be found unsatisfactory. For Ghanaians, the real issue is not who comes to invest per se. Malaysians have developed their country into a very beautiful one. Unfortunately, when they came to Ghana, they did not develop Ghana as it was hoped they would. Ghanaians must wake up to the realisation that the days of the foreign charitable Missionaries who built the schools, hospitals, roads are long gone, and that just handing over one's vital entities to a "competent" investor without proper structures and regulation will not produce the desired results. Whilst it is critical that whoever comes to invest in Ghana has a track record (something that the neophyte Consortium led by the Malaysian Telecommunications Company did not have), it is far more important how we regulate the investor, and make them conform to high standards of telecom service delivery."

Quality/Reliability

"We Must Get Our Telephones Working!", *Accra Mail*, May 2002

"Have you ever tried making a call from 021 to any of the mobile phone lines in the country? At best it is time consuming and at worst so frustrating that you give up altogether. We cannot pretend that things are normal in this sector. Things are getting from bad to worse and unless some fast and imaginative improvements are made, the entire sector would collapse before long.

"At first many Ghanaians thought the Malaysians in charge of Ghana Telecom were the main culprits — which they may well be, or not — but after months of showing them the red card, we cannot say with any certainty that we have seen any improvements in the service of GT nor for that matter, any of the mobile phone operators. Nor do we see any light at the end of the tunnel in terms of who is stepping into the shoes of the Malaysians. We are concerned because an efficient telecom system is absolutely necessary for modern business and commerce. The President has promised Ghanaians a 'Golden Age of Business'. If there is one sector that would be crucial to the attainment of this objective, it must be the telecom sector. If ordinary citizens are so frustrated with the sector, can we imagine the despair that big business can be suffering? Time we are told is money and no business concern would like to invest or expand in a country where poor telecommunications can lead to loss of time and loss of money."

Failure of Privatisation Due to Lack of Political Commitment and Weak Regulatory Frameworks: Lessons from Case Studies

Political commitment is a crucial issue when considering privatisation in infrastructure, and more specifically in the power and water sectors, which remain highly monopolistic. A lack of enforcement capability may lead to strategic renegotiations or termination of contracts on the part of private operators or governments. On this issue, the Inter-American Development Bank has developed an original data set describing the characteristics of nearly 1 000 infrastructure projects (mainly concession contracts) awarded in Latin American and Caribbean countries from 1989 to 2000 in the telecommunications, energy, transport and water sectors. Using this database, Guash *et al.* (2002) perform econometric tests on the determinants of contract renegotiations, confirming several theoretically-based intuitions. In particular, they suggest that fewer contracts (especially strategic ones) are renegotiated under conditions of better institutional quality (e.g. the rule of law, lack of corruption and the quality of bureaucracy) combined with the existence of a regulator.

Case Studies in the Power Sector

The privatisation of the Société Nationale d'Electricité (Sonel) in Cameroon and of the Société Nationale d'Electricité du Sénégal (Sénélec) are relevant examples of privatisations that failed owing to inadequacies in political commitment and the regulatory framework. By contrast, the successful privatisation of Côte d'Ivoire's power company CIE presents an interesting case of strong political commitment engendering full local ownership of the reform.

AES/Sonel: no preparation phase and no restructuring prior to privatisation

The process of privatising Sonel started in 1995 and was completed in February 2001, when AES Sirocco was granted a concession licence with a 51 per cent stake in Sonel for $30.5 million. The concession licence granted AES-Sonel a 20-year monopoly over the generation, transmission and distribution of electricity, while infrastructure — including new infrastructure to be built during the concession period — remained state-owned. Since then, however, power cuts, price increases and retrenchments have become the rule, creating huge resentment among the population. AES-Sonel Director Mark Miller has been nicknamed the "Dark Killer" on account of the tragic fires caused by candles used during blackouts.

It seems, however, that such dysfunctions are due less to mismanagement on the part of AES Sirocco than to a blatant lack of political commitment in the privatisation process. The fact is that the facilities sold to AES-Sonel were obsolete, because the government had been neglecting the maintenance of infrastructure. Over the years, the production capacity of the three hydro-electric dams has fallen substantially. The Edea dam, built in 1952 and never renovated since, hardly generates enough electricity to supply Alucam, a Pechiney subsidiary. Similarly, the Song-Loulou dam has not been renovated for 30 years, while that of Lagdo generates only one-third of its nominal capacity. Moreover, the financial difficulties that AES faces in the United States (following the Enron scandal) may jeopardise the company's commitment to invest a total of $500 million over a 20-year period. These difficulties drove AES-Sonel in April 2002 to announce a rate increase each year for the following five years so as to "improve its viability and offer a high-quality service". It is doubtful, however, that these increases will be enough to enable AES-Sonel to reach its objectives. Moreover, the differing views of AES-Sonel and the government, combined with the discontent of both trade unions (which expect staff reductions ranging from 2 500 to 3 900 employees) and consumers (the first victims of power cuts), could prevent such a decision from being accepted.

Sénélec: the lack of a regulatory framework was denounced by the new political coalition, leading to the re-nationalisation of the company

The lack of a common point of view between the government and private investors was also at the root of the failure of the privatisation of Sénélec in Senegal. Sénélec was privatised in 1998 by the socialist government in power at the time and was transferred to a strategic partner (the French-Canadian consortium Elyo/Hydro-Québec) without any proper regulatory framework. Consequently, the reform lacked legitimacy among the population and in political circles. In September 2000, considering that the consortium had not honoured its commitments, the new government decided to breach the contract. It reimbursed the consortium $62 million in exchange for the re-nationalisation of Sénélec, and a new public call for tenders was launched in July 2001.

Although President Abdoulaye Wade considered a tariff increase as a possible option, however, the failure to undertake deep restructuring of the sector made it very doubtful that a contract with another private investor would be sustainable. As a matter of fact, although the new tender saw Vivendi-ONE (Office National d'Electricité) and AES arrive first and second respectively in November 2001, less than one year later both candidates had decided to withdraw. In February 2002, Vivendi breached its contract, refusing to pay the agreed sum of nearly $90 million for the purchase of a 51 per cent stake in Sénélec, because it would have been obliged to invest a further $245 million to build a new power station and renovate the obsolete transmission and distribution grid. The public tender process launched a year earlier came to an end when AES, in turn, officially declined to purchase Sénélec in July 2002, owing to major cash difficulties and management problems at Sonel, its power company in Cameroon.

The Senegalese authorities have thus retained the ownership of Sénélec, but the recurrent failure of the privatisation process has drawn their attention to the need to restructure the power sector before undertaking deeper reforms. After the withdrawal of Vivendi in February 2002, the government unilaterally decided to raise prices by 10 per cent to counterbalance the damaging consequences of the botched privatisation and to upgrade infrastructure in order to bring down the worrying rate of power shortages. The tariff increases will not, however, be sufficient to cover the costs of restructuring. As of July 2002, the Senegalese government had already spent $160 million to re-nationalise Sénélec and to finance structural inefficiencies in the distribution network. The former energy sector investment policy is now strongly criticised by the current government, which claims that Sénélec's power shortages and financial deficit are due to the purchase of gas turbines: the fuel used in such turbines costs twice as much as the fuels commonly used in power stations, driving Sénélec to spend 60 per cent of its turnover on fuel instead of 30 per cent. To avoid bankruptcy, the government therefore had to inject an additional $56 million, and a further $42 million was spent on subsidies to lower fuel costs and avoid large tariff increases. In short, the case of Sénélec shows how costly the lack of regulation can be.

CIE: a privatisation carried out at the initiative of the Ivorian government without pressure from international donors, reflecting a strong political commitment to reform

In contrast, the privatisation of the power sector in Côte d'Ivoire in 1990 illustrates the outstanding results that can be obtained when strong political commitment is combined with tight co-ordination between government and the private investor and an appropriate regulatory framework. The privatisation was neither imposed nor recommended by international donors, but unilaterally "demanded" by President Houphouët-Boigny in order to improve a sector which was already performing quite well compared to other African countries, but which showed around 50 hours of power cuts per year and a total debt equivalent to €7 billion (CFAF 230 billion). Thus, the Compagnie Ivoirienne d'Electricité (CIE) was founded, with EDF-SAUR taking a 51 per cent stake on the basis of a 15-year concession for power distribution, renewable for 20 years. One year after the privatisation, CIE had already invested CFAF 12 billion to upgrade the network, which had been neglected since independence, even forcing Côte d'Ivoire to import power from Ghana. At the same time, the company had already recorded net income of CFAF 700 million, as against a deficit of CFAF 70 billion before privatisation. The billing system was also restructured, and emphasis was put on staff training and quality of service, while those who did not pay their bills (especially the wealthier consumers) were deprived of power. Though potentially damaging for lower-income domestic consumers, these first measures rapidly proved to be progressive, as the tariff increases at the end of the process were very low. For instance, the renovation of facilities led to a 60 per cent reduction in the number of power cuts, while the number of subscribers grew by 50 per cent. At the end of 1997, total investments amounted to CFAF 49 billion (showing that the private investors had honoured their engagements), and taxes and fees paid to government reached CFAF 277 billion. Sales revenue amounted to CFAF 170 billion, of which 30 per cent stemmed from export activities. Two new power stations were built.

Twelve years after the privatisation, the outcome appears to be highly positive, with figures described by observers as "amazing": the number of subscribers has doubled and now stands at 800 000. Total sales have also doubled to reach CFAF 192.7 billion. The CIE staff has grown by 20 per cent, domestic power consumption by 64 per cent and total power generation by 17 per cent. The privatisation of the power sector seems to have benefited both consumers, with an average cost per KWh that increased by only CFAF 10 from 1994 to 2001, and the state, which has enjoyed substantial fiscal revenues. These very positive results should make the renegotiation of the contract in 2005 relatively smooth.

Case Studies in the Water Sector

Privatisation in the water sector requires even stronger political commitment and regulatory frameworks, owing to the strategic status of water provision in developing countries. The course of water privatisation in Guinea followed a pattern very similar to that of Senegal's electric power sector and Ghana's telecom sector, in that the lack of a regulatory framework led to poor performance on the part of the private operator. As a result, Guinea's water company SEEG was re-nationalised in 2001 after the failure of efforts to negotiate a new 15-year lease contract with SAUR. Although such contract terminations are very costly and result from the absence of a real independent regulatory authority, they are a signal that sub-Saharan governments are moving forward on the regulatory "learning curve". Indeed, it seems that some of them are entering what Kayizzi-Mugerwa (2002) calls the "fully fledged" phase, that is, the last step in the learning process (see Box 1). In this phase, the government has learned from blatant failures in the past and become aware of the need to make adjustments, and in particular to strengthen the legal framework. The water privatisation operations in Côte d'Ivoire (SODECI) and Senegal (DEG) bear more resemblance to the privatisation of the Ivorian power company CIE, where there was a genuine political commitment to establishing a satisfactory regulatory framework. As in every lease contract, however, it was difficult in both cases to create clearly separate bodies responsible respectively for investment and maintenance.

The catastrophic outcome of the privatisation of municipal water networks in South Africa offers a clear illustration of the consequences of inadequate regulation. This failure can be attributed to four main causes: the small size and very low standard of living of the population in the areas, the difficulty experienced by municipalities in establishing a proper regulatory framework, their lack of credibility and enforcement capacity, and the opportunities for corruption, which found very fertile ground because of the small and isolated scale of the networks.

From 1999 to 2001, three water privatisation transactions were implemented locally. Of these, the 30-year concession contract signed between SAUR and the resort of Dolphin Coast in 1999 is instructive regarding the difficulties water privatisation encounters in South Africa. The Dolphin Coast resort in Kwazulu Natal (population 56 000) is mostly composed of peri-urban villages. The motivation to privatise water services stemmed from the municipalities' lack of capacity and ability to raise funds to finance investments. However, this inability to run water services properly meant that they were also unable properly to regulate the new private operator, i.e. to reconcile profitability and distributional objectives. Moreover, privatising relatively small areas where the majority of people are poor prevents the private investor from making profits and complicates the task of decision makers. In the event, the price increases led to riots and to a massive refusal on the part of consumers to pay their bills.

The combination of the lack of a regulatory framework and the very poor potential of the market for the private investor led the company into financial difficulties in 2001. In April 2001, Siza Water refused to pay the scheduled R3.6 million lease payment due to one of the Dolphin Coast municipalities. The private investors had been interested in the project subject to very substantial development of middle-income and mass housing, but the actual figures were far below what was expected, causing Siza's revenue to drop by about R12 million a year. The contract was then renegotiated: water prices were increased by 15 per cent to restore profitability, while the investments required of Siza were reduced from R25 million to R10 million.

Development of Financial Markets and the "Ownership Indigenisation" Process

Privatisation has often been considered as a way to promote the development of capital markets and stock exchanges through the flotation of former state-owned companies. This is seen as ultimately favouring the development of the national private sector through the participation of local investors in the process (often referred to as the "indigenisation" process, i.e. the transfer of economic power to the local population). However, the empirical evidence seems ambiguous regarding the achievement of such objectives. The "indigenisation" process is still under-developed, especially where the privatisation of network utilities is concerned. It should be noted, however, that South Africa is a special case, as "ownership indigenisation" has become a priority there as part of the drive for black economic empowerment.

Figure 16. **Number of Privatisations through Public Flotation**

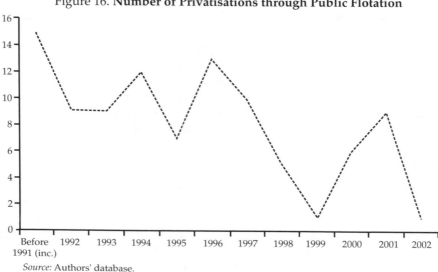

Source: Authors' database.

Figure 17. **Nationality of SOEs Privatised Through Flotation**

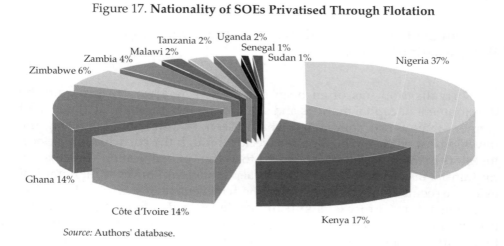

Source: Authors' database.

Development of Financial Markets

Since the beginning of the process in 1990, the number of privatisations through public flotation has been limited, amounting to only 97 transactions out of a total of 2 535 (3.8 per cent). Moreover, the trend is clearly downward (see Figure 16), which confirms the difficulties experienced by African countries in building stock exchanges and capital markets. Although one listing can be enough to "launch" stock exchange activities in a country, it offers no guarantee of numerous further listings on this exchange.

According to Figure 17, Nigerian, Kenyan, Ivorian and Ghanaian companies represent 81 per cent of the former SOEs now listed on stock exchanges. This predominance is mainly due to the fact that these countries had relatively well developed stock markets prior to the listing of the first former SOEs. In the last few years, however, some other stock exchanges have developed under the pressure of the privatisation process, and this has sometimes led to cross-listings, thereby helping to consolidate regional stock markets. The stock exchanges referred to here often have a market capitalisation of less than $100 million, making Africa the continent with the highest concentration of new, small stock markets.

Local Stock Exchanges

The Nigerian Stock Exchange, established in 1960, is clearly emerging as one of the leading exchanges in sub-Saharan Africa, with a total market capitalisation of $6.82 billion as of 10 March 2003. Of the 260 companies listed, 26 are former SOEs (mainly in the financial sector) privatised in the early 1990s. There has been no recent flotation of lately privatised SOEs, however, showing that, even on a dynamic stock exchange, privatisation through flotation is far from common.

The Nairobi Stock Exchange (NSE) in Kenya, established in 1954, is much smaller than the Nigerian exchange but has played an important role in the Kenyan economy where the privatisation of SOEs is concerned. The first privatisation through the NSE was the successful sale of the government's 20 per cent stake in Kenya Commercial Bank, in which the issue was over-subscribed by a factor of 2.3. Since then, the largest share issue in the history of the NSE was the privatisation of Kenya Airways in 1996 (listed simultaneously on the NSE and the London Stock Exchange). In 1996, the Kenya Airways privatisation team obtained the World Bank Award for Excellence as the authors of a model success story in the divestiture of state-owned enterprises. The operation enabled Kenyan institutions and individuals to acquire 34 per cent of the shares issued and international investors 14 per cent. The airline's employees were able to enrol in a special programme to purchase 3 per cent of the shares. Overall, as many as 110 000 different shareholders have participated in the domestic offering.

The Abidjan Stock Exchange (Bourse des Valeurs d'Abidjan), established in 1974, was the only stock exchange in French-speaking West Africa until its transformation into a regional stock exchange (Bourse Régionale des Valeurs Mobilières, or BRVM) in 1998. This new exchange was supposed to bring together the member countries of the West African Economic and Monetary Union (WAEMU): Benin, Burkina Faso, Côte d'Ivoire, Guinea-Bissau, Mali, Niger, Senegal and Togo. Initially, 35 Ivorian companies were listed on the BRVM (including 14 former SOEs), amounting to a total capitalisation of $5.14 billion. The listing of the first non-Ivorian company (the Senegalese telecommunications group Sonatel), also in 1998, raised the total market capitalisation by more than 20 per cent. The 17 per cent stake in Sonatel offered for public sale was considerably over-subscribed; two-thirds of this block of shares were reserved for Senegalese nationals and institutions, leading to the participation of 9 000 Senegalese individuals who paid a total of CFAF 17 billion ($30 million). This came as a surprise, as little individual participation had been expected owing to Senegal's generally low saving rate. Since then, Sonatel shares have risen in value and traded briskly on the Abidjan exchange, dwarfing almost all other stocks. According to Azam *et al.* (2002), Sonatel shares account for about 25 per cent of the capitalised quotation on the BRVM. Recently, Sonatel has further contributed to the development of the stock exchange through a bond issue worth CFAF 12 billion ($17 million) to finance the modernisation of its network over the 2000-2004 period. In 2001/2002, Sonatel shares offered high returns to investors thanks to the company's exceptional financial performance.

The Ghana Stock Exchange (GSE) was founded in July 1989 and trading began in 1990. It has been the third-largest exchange in sub-Saharan Africa since 1994, when 30 per cent of the government's shares in the Ashanti Goldfields Corporation were listed on both the GSE and the London Stock Exchange. This privatisation, still regarded as the largest ever conducted in sub-Saharan Africa (excluding the Telkom transaction in South Africa), enabled the GSE to raise $1.8 billion (around 90 per cent of its total capitalisation in 1994). Since then, successful privatisations have been carried out in the brewing and financial sectors. In particular, the formerly state-owned Ghana

Commercial Bank (listed on the GSE in 1996) became the best performer on the GSE in 2002, with final dividends of $7.5 million and an after-tax profit of $22.67 million. Consequently, although it hosts only 16 per cent of the former SOEs in sub-Saharan Africa, the GSE seems by far the most dynamic stock exchange of the four discussed here. This should be confirmed following the Ghanaian government's announcement in January 2003 that the most viable of the ten SOEs earmarked for privatisation would be divested through the GSE.

Recent Trends

Since 1996, only 45 former SOEs have been listed on stock markets in sub-Saharan Africa. Some of these, however, have contributed greatly to the launching of capital market activities in the countries concerned. In Malawi, for instance, the stock exchange first opened for business on 11 November 1996, with the listing of Malawi's largest insurance firm, the National Insurance Company. Since then, eight other successful operations have been carried out (including two former SOEs). As a result, whereas in 1996 the MSE traded 258 600 shares having a total value of $6.5 million, by the close of 2001 the number of traded shares had risen to almost 183 million with a total value of about $15.9 million.

Stock exchanges that have initially been boosted by the flotation of former SOEs do not always show such growth. On the Lusaka Stock Exchange, whose listings were triggered by Zambia's privatisation process, the failed privatisation of Konkola Copper Mines and the poor performance of the economy led to a drop in market capitalisation and trading activities, which shows the vulnerability of African capital markets.

The most recently established stock exchanges are the Uganda Securities Exchange (USE), which opened in January 1998, and the Dar es Salaam Stock Exchange (DSE), which began trading in March 1998. Both were initially driven by the flotation of a state-owned company (Uganda Clays Ltd and Tanzania Oxygen Ltd), but these listings have not been followed by other sizeable ones, owing to a lack of interest (and sometimes investment capacity) on the part of both foreign and local investors. This led the USE and the DSE to link their activities to those of the NSE so as to strengthen their respective positions. In March 2002, this "regionalisation" trend took the form of the cross-listing of Kenya Airways Ltd on the USE (whose market capitalisation thereby rose from $143 million to $193 million), providing an opportunity for local stakeholders to own shares of a successful regional company. This operation was not the first cross-listing of a former SOE to occur in sub-Saharan Africa. In 2000, Sudatel became the first company not a member of the Gulf Cooperation Council (GCC) to be listed on the Bahrain Stock Exchange (in addition to its initial listing on the Khartoum Stock Exchange, or KSE), with an authorised capital of $250 million. This operation, the biggest since the inception of the KSE in 1994, considerably expanded the capital market in Sudan and increased the KSE's market capitalisation from $44 million in 1995 to $400 million at end 2000, with 44 companies listed. Given these positive examples, cross-listing of former SOEs is likely to develop further in the future. This practice not only allows local investors to buy shares in successful regional companies, but also favours reciprocal investments, which are more acceptable to the population because they are more balanced.

In sum, the evidence suggests that privatisation has helped to develop capital markets in sub-Saharan Africa, either by "launching" them (as in Malawi, Uganda and Tanzania) or by diversifying their activities and products through initial public offerings (IPOs) aimed at encouraging savings and increasing the investment awareness of both individuals and companies. As of end 2002, securities exchanges had been established in 16 sub-Saharan countries, including Botswana, Ghana, Kenya, Malawi, Mauritius, Mozambique, Namibia, Nigeria, South Africa, Sudan, Swaziland, Tanzania, Uganda, Zambia and Zimbabwe. The development of the Johannesburg Stock Exchange (JSE) is not mentioned in our analysis because no privatisation operations in South Africa involved listing on the stock exchange until the Telkom IPO in March 2003. In contrast to the JSE, however, which has a market capitalisation of $215 billion, many African stock markets remain very small and thus highly illiquid. Even on relatively dynamic stock exchanges like that of Ghana, only a very few of the 22 companies listed see daily trading activity. Consequently, the IPOs triggered by the privatisation process have not been followed by significant new transactions, owing to the reluctance of privately-held companies to enter an illiquid market. Moreover, the number of privatisations through public flotation has decreased over the last ten years because IPOs on such stock markets are successful only if the company is highly viable and thus likely to be over-subscribed by local and foreign investors. This condition is obviously not always met, since, as was pointed out above, companies are often privatised because of their structural inefficiencies.

Capital markets are still often used by governments to raise loan finance rather than to mobilise capital for industry. This use of capital markets by states with relatively low creditworthiness leads to a lack of public confidence in the integrity of securities markets, constituting a major obstacle to stock exchange development in Africa. Odife (2000) also points to deep popular mistrust of financial institutions owing to past episodes of mismanagement of banks and funds. Such mistrust naturally leads to inefficient allocation of savings, which are not placed in financial institutions. Consequently, among the principal measures to be taken to improve business confidence, Odife suggests:

1. **Cross-listing of securities on exchanges** (already initiated in the case of former SOEs): such a scheme helps to enhance confidence by spreading risk and control over several countries and improving the reputation of the securities concerned.

2. **The adoption of "merit review" standards by securities agencies**: merit reviews improve both the transparency and the visibility of listed companies by screening offerings and making public the list of top performers.

3. **Increasing the media's understanding of and reporting on business matters** will similarly improve transparency, as such reporting is seen as a trustworthy guarantee from non-biased sources.

4. **Increasing the enforcement authority of government agencies** so as to allow for better and more credible oversight.

5. **Expanding capacity for institutional trading through pension and retirement funds** in order to attract savings to the financial market and offer security.

Broadening Local Participation

Broadening local ownership is frequently cited as a major objective of privatisation by African governments. With few exceptions, however, only minor efforts have been made in this direction, as is indicated by the marginal use of methods that are supposed to broaden local participation, such as public flotation, management/employee buyouts and trustees.

Public Flotation

Public flotation has accounted for less than 4 per cent of the number of privatisations in sub-Saharan Africa since the mid-1980s. Some of these operations, however, have broadened company ownership and promoted the transfer of economic power to the local population. For instance, the privatisation of Kenya Airways in 1996 enabled Kenyan institutions and individuals to acquire 34 per cent of the shares issued. In Malawi, the privatisation of the National Insurance Company (the first company to be listed) allowed 2 300 Malawian citizens to buy shares. On the Lusaka Stock Exchange, domestic investors have kept the market going, with about 20 000 Zambians investing in the stock market in 2000, as against fewer than 1 000 in 1994.

This broadening of ownership has been enhanced by regulations giving priority to local investors. In Ghana, for instance, there are restrictions on non-resident portfolio investors, although such investors can deal in securities listed on the exchange without obtaining prior permission from the exchange control authority. On the Dar es Salaam exchange, foreign investors are simply barred from trading. Such restrictions are far from widespread, however, and do not apply to the largest stock exchanges, which considerably limits their effects. Moreover, stock market development is still in its infancy, which impedes the process of "indigenisation" through public flotation, with the exception of South Africa.

The reason for this exception is that South Africa has institutionalised the concept of "black empowerment", defined as political and economic measures aiming at favouring "historically disadvantaged individuals" ("those who, over the years of colonialism and apartheid, had been denied and stripped of their right to wealth") so as to give them access to property. A recent example of such a measure is a special offer (the Khulisa offer) for the initial listing of Telkom shares on the JSE in March 2003. The Khulisa offer consisted in targeting low-income earners by proposing a lock-up period of three months, an individual participation cap of R5 000 ($725) and a loyalty bonus for individuals who retained their shares for at least two years. On the first day of quotation, 127 000 South Africans invested in Telkom, 60 per cent of them through the Khulisa offer. The Telkom IPO (the first IPO of a public enterprise in South Africa, as mentioned above) should thus be considered as the first real success of the black empowerment strategy, since, according to the empowerment rating agency Empowerdex, in late 2002 black investors controlled less than 10 per cent of the JSE. Moreover, the Khulisa offer for the first time took the debate beyond the narrow issue of "colour" by specifically targeting lower-income people. However, this initiative has not met with unanimous approval: the partial privatisation of Telkom in 1997 led to increases in tariffs that, according to members of the Congress of South African Trade Unions (COSATU), will not be compensated by the discounted price and other advantages of the Khulisa offer.

114

Management/Employee Buyouts, Trustees and Employee Shareholding

Management/employee buyouts, defined as the acquisition by management or employees of the shares or principal assets of an enterprise, have been surprisingly rare in Africa, accounting for less than 1.5 per cent of transactions to end 2002. To our knowledge, only Burundi, Cape Verde, Gambia, Kenya, Sao Tome & Principe, Tanzania, Uganda and Zambia have witnessed such operations, with Zambia accounting for 50 per cent of the cases. According to Makonnen (1999), the Zambian government was eager to encourage employee participation in 1995 and identified 30 public enterprises that were suitable candidates for management/employee buyouts. Only five such buyouts were actually concluded, however, owing to unrealistic business plans that relied too heavily on support from government or banks and made inadequate allowance for much-needed investment.

The use of "trustees" (very similar to "directed group ownership") has been minimal, accounting for less than 1 per cent of transactions. Only five countries (Burkina Faso, Mali, Tanzania, Uganda and Zambia) made use of this method, generally with the intention of demonstrating the government's commitment to transferring ownership to indigenous investors. In 1995, with the privatisation of the Ugandan Tea Grower's Corporation, this technique made it possible, for the first time in Africa, to involve farmers directly in the privatisation process.

Employee shareholding is very similar to a sale of shares and may occur as part of a negotiated sale of shares to private investors or alongside a public flotation, when a small block of shares is reserved for employees. The latter option was chosen in the case of the privatisation of Kenya Airways: airline employees were offered an opportunity to enrol in a special programme to purchase 3 per cent of the issued shares. Similarly, when a 29 per cent stake in the Compagnie Ivoirienne d'Electricité (CIE) was floated in 1992, 5 per cent was reserved for employees. Finally, the public flotation of a 27 per cent stake of Sonatel on the BRVM in 1998 allowed Sonatel employees to buy 10 per cent of the shares at a highly discounted rate, easing some of the workers' earlier anxieties about privatisation. Although employee shareholding is politically attractive, it can cause difficulties for policy makers. For instance, it often makes deal negotiations longer and may significantly reduce the price of shares, which explains why this technique is not widely used to foster ownership indigenisation.

This review of the methods used to broaden ownership suggests that only limited efforts have been made to achieve the objective of "ownership indigenisation". This lack of political will (often combined with a lack of transparency) is particularly evident when one considers that privatisations conducted on an uncompetitive basis account for almost 14 per cent of total transactions (excluding liquidations), which shows that selling to existing shareholders having pre-emptive rights have been particularly widespread (in Kenya, for instance, such sales represent 70 per cent of privatisation transactions prior to 1995). Moreover, while privatisations conducted on a competitive basis have the notable virtue of maximising the sale value, they are often regarded as the enemy of ownership indigenisation, since they generally exclude local investors from the bidding process. The exceptions include countries such as Mali, Nigeria and Kenya, where local businessmen have managed to some extent to resist the pressure from foreign investors.

Main Obstacles to the Broadening of Local Participation

The emergence of a sound private sector is also constrained by the fact that local investors involved in the privatisation process encounter major bottlenecks such as poor management capabilities and lack of access to cheap financing for further investment. Lack of know-how is one of the main causes of bankruptcy among small and medium-sized enterprises acquired by local actors, as highlighted in the case of Mozambique. Over the years, programmes providing technical training and financial assistance have been launched by the government to involve more Mozambican investors in the privatisation process and make privately-owned Mozambican firms more competitive. One of these, the Fund to Support Economic Rehabilitation (FARE), implemented in 1996, used some of the proceeds from privatisation to provide loans to micro-enterprises, but this programme has had only a very limited impact. More recently, the Ministry of Industry and Trade and the World Bank launched another project to foster the development of national enterprises (PoDE). It identifies two main areas of assistance: technical and financial. While the technical assistance component, which is funded on a 50 per cent cost-sharing basis by the government and the company involved, has brought positive results so far, the credit line to small and medium-sized enterprises is not working well because it lacks guarantee schemes and because the market interest rates charged are too high.

Where credit constraints are concerned, although financial services have been expanding in recent years, mainly through greater foreign involvement, many firms face enormous difficulties in borrowing working capital because of the unfavourable macroeconomic environment (i.e. high interest rates). Only firms with relatively easy access to capital in other markets, such as South Africa, can overcome the high cost of capital. Thus, the financial policy environment seems to be tilted in favour of foreign investors rather than national entrepreneurs, and the fiscal environment in many countries shows the same bias in the provision of tax incentives or exemptions. This bias towards foreign investors is particularly evident in the case of utilities, where the main shareholders are always foreign investors, and often multinationals from the former colonial powers (as shown in the tables presenting privatisations in the telecom, power and water sectors). This involvement creates great resentment among the population, which considers such foreign direct investment as pure neo-colonialism. This explains the very vocal campaigns organised against the privatisation of utilities (especially water).

Some studies argue that local private participation has been hindered by large-scale projects that demand heavy capital investment, which dissuades local investors. In the long term, limited local involvement may neutralise the positive outcomes of the reform, mainly because there will not be a significant group of local stakeholders to promote the industrialisation of the country. The only country that has attempted to create small and medium-sized entities in the power sector is Mauritius, where according to Karekezi and Kimani (2002) close to 25 per cent of annual electricity generation comes from local privately owned and operated cogeneration plants in the sugar industry. The technology involved has been easily mastered by local entrepreneurs, and the capital requirements have been modest and therefore sourced locally. However, this remains an isolated case.

It is vital for governments to strengthen their efforts to promote local participation in the privatisation process. The desire of local populations to defend their sovereignty and legitimately to appropriate the benefits of privatisation is very strong and easily understandable, but stock markets in Africa, which could help broaden local participation in the long term, are still in their infancy. An alternative medium-term solution could be methods such as "directed group participation" for privatisation in competitive sectors, as they seem to have been successful in countries like Uganda. One way to make the privatisation of utilities politically acceptable might be the development of "pre-emptive rights equivalents" for residents. This was done in 1996 during the second stage of the privatisation of Cabo Verde Telecom, where 20 per cent of the capital was reserved to Cape Verdeans: 5 per cent was sold to employees of the telecom operator, 15 per cent to local private investors and 5 per cent to Cape Verdeans living abroad.

It is doubtful, however, if such measures are sufficient to win popular acceptance of strategic privatisation in utilities. They must be necessarily accompanied by an appropriate regulatory framework that clearly defines the rules governing the private/public partnership so as to prevent abuses on the part of the private investor. Building an efficient regulatory framework takes time and requires political reforms, however, starting with measures against endemic corruption and non-transparent practices.

Notes

1. Data from the OECD privatisation database, excluding the Slovak Republic, for which data are not available, and Luxembourg, where no privatisation has occurred.

2. From the OECD Development Centre questionnaire submitted to the Privatisation Agency in June 2002.

3. The larger decline in dollar terms is due to the devaluation of the CFA franc in January 1994.

4. Fixed-line penetration is equivalent to "main-line penetration" or "teledensity". A fixed line is defined by the ITU as "a telephone line connecting the subscriber's terminal equipment to the public switched network and which has a dedicated port in the telephone exchange equipment".

Chapter 3

Policy Conclusions: The Impact on the Poor?

Overview of the Privatisation Process in Africa

Privatisation is now part and parcel of the reform agenda of most African economies. Thirty-eight countries in sub-Saharan Africa have already implemented privatisation programmes, some of them from the late 1980s or early 1990s. While most privatisations of small and medium-sized enterprises in the competitive sector took place in the early 1990s, it was only in the second half of the 1990s that the privatisation process started to involve larger enterprises, including, in recent years, companies in the network utilities sector.

The process was driven by several forces, including budgetary concerns. The sale of assets was aimed at raising immediate revenue for the government and solving the inability of the state to finance needed expenditures on new investment and/or maintenance. Privatisation was also driven by the need to stop subsidising SOEs in order to release resources for other pressing public expenditure and to overcome the poor performance of state-run utilities in terms of high costs, inadequate expansion of access to services for the poor and/or unreliable supply.

The privatisation process has proceeded at a much slower pace in sub-Saharan Africa than in other regions, and it is still incomplete. According to information collected by the African Economic Outlook team of the OECD Development Centre on some 48 sub-Saharan countries in 2002, in at least half of the countries the water, fixed-line telephone, railway transportation, air transportation and petroleum product distribution sectors were still state-owned, while in more than two-thirds of the countries, SOEs in the electrical power generation and distribution sector had not been privatised. These figures suggest significant delays in the reform of utilities and regulated services.

Admittedly, privatising public utilities is more complex than privatising companies in competitive sectors. The different nature and larger scope of utilities requires the simultaneous creation of regulatory authorities. However, the available data suggest that not all SOEs earmarked for privatisation in competitive sectors have been privatised either. According to our data, many privatisations are still pending: some 330 companies, or 13 per cent of the number already privatised. This proportion is higher than 20 per cent in 16 countries and higher than 33 per cent in 10 countries.

Overall, the reasons for the limited results compared to the ambitious agenda of privatisation lie in the difficulties encountered in preparing for and implementing the process. In the first place, time is required to design a proper regulatory framework to guarantee a smooth transition. In many instances, the privatisation programme also suffers from the incompetence of the privatisation agencies appointed. In others, vested interests played a major role in retaining the so-called "strategic companies" in the hands of the state, leading to the postponement of the privatisation plan. The reluctance of governments to sell companies in some vital sectors of the economy and in the utilities sector often resulted in neglect of the economic situation of SOEs, which became increasingly unproductive, inefficient, overstaffed and characterised by bad management and corruption. Postponement of privatisation accompanied by the deteriorating situation of some SOEs led local and foreign investors to adopt a wait-and-see attitude, which ultimately exacerbated governments' difficulties in attracting potential investors.

The lack of political consensus on privatisation policies, a poor regulatory framework in certain instances and a general lack of capacity have led in a number of cases to reversal of privatisation. Strategic companies had to be re-nationalised, either because they proved to be unprofitable or because private investors proved unable to comply with their contractual obligations. In Zambia, for instance the government renationalised Konkola Copper Mines (KCM), which accounts for about two-thirds of the country's copper production. KCM was sold in 2000 to the Anglo-American Corporation at a highly discounted price, mainly because of the obsolescence of the plant. After incurring substantial losses due to the inherited poor state of the plant, Anglo-American pulled out in 2002. Another example of re-nationalisation is found in Senegal. The national electric power company, Sénélec, was privatised in

1998 by the socialist government in office at the time and was transferred to a strategic partner, the French-Canadian consortium Elyo/Hydro-Québec, without any proper regulatory framework. Consequently, the reform lacked legitimacy both in the eyes of the public and in political circles. In September 2000, considering that the consortium had not honoured its commitments, the new government decided to breach the contract, reimbursing $62 million to the consortium in exchange for the re-nationalisation of Sénélec.

Public opinion is another important reason for the postponement of many privatisation policies. The general hostility of the public has been based on fear of employee layoffs, price increases and the perception that the benefits and the distributional impact of privatisation are long in coming. In many countries, the commencement of the privatisation process has led to riots and protracted political debate. In July 2002, for instance, thousands of Burkinabè workers went on strike and demonstrated against privatisation and the 5 200 job cuts the unions claimed it entailed.

The concern of the public is that privatisation, despite its potential positive economic impact, may have an adverse social impact. It is true that several dimensions need to be taken into account when assessing privatisation. In the context of Africa, the ultimate question is whether the process has benefited the poor. The impact of privatisation on poverty may be positive or negative, depending on the circumstances and on the way the privatisation policy is implemented. The following sections summarise our previous findings on privatisation with a focus on its possible consequences for poverty.

Fiscal Impact

Privatisation transactions are often considered detrimental to the poor because they entail the elimination of subsidies to products and services needed by the poor, such as water, electricity and public transportation. The question, however, is whether such goods and services are best subsidised through state involvement in their production. When public money is saved through privatisation, this money may be made available to invest in poverty-targeted projects. What is achieved by privatisation is essentially a clarification of the role of the state, in which opaque subsidy mechanisms are replaced by more transparent accounting of public expenditure.

It is very often impossible to evaluate the fiscal impact of privatisation precisely, because the subsidies given to SOEs before privatisation were not well identified in the government budget. Governments and the international agencies supporting their reform programmes should make a greater effort clearly to identify the fiscal resources saved through privatisation, and to channel these resources to poverty-targeted expenditure. In the context of a sub-Saharan African country, privatisation policies should not be designed with the sole objective of reducing public expenditure or collecting money through privatisation receipts; rather, the aim should be to reorganise such expenditure in order to fight poverty more efficiently. But this is not easily done when there is no clear evaluation of the net resources added to the budget through a privatisation transaction (including the proceeds of the sale, the elimination of subsidies and broadening of the tax base) and of the amount of subsidies the poor actually enjoyed before privatisation.

Moreover, it should be recognised that not all subsidies to SOEs are geared to reduce poverty, mainly because those who have access to the services concerned are the richest groups. In many instances, public enterprises have been used to secure rents to a relatively small clientele, offering either above-market wages or under-pricing for those with access. Indeed, the blanket nature of many subsidies makes them poorly targeted. In Uganda, for instance, 94 per cent of the population in 1995 was effectively subsidising the 6 per cent who had access to electricity, in the amount of $50 million a year. In urban areas of Ethiopia in 1996, around 86 per cent of subsidies on kerosene were captured by the non-poor, since kerosene consumption increases with income.

Furthermore, even when significant rates of subsidies are applied on the official market, many poor people are forced to buy from secondary markets (because of lack of legal access), and the benefits of low official prices are also enjoyed by the rich. The fact is that consumption subsidies do not appear to be crucial to making energy resources accessible to the poor: the cost of access to electricity is related to up-front fixed costs that are not subsidised and that are affordable by the urban poor only if they have access to credit or if these initial costs are spread over the lifetime of the infrastructure concerned.

Impact on Prices

There is widespread concern that cuts in subsidies might be socially damaging because they lead to price increases. The evidence shows that such price increases are not systematic, however, and in fact are highly dependent on the specific characteristics of the sector. In the case of telecommunications, prices may actually be pushed downwards because the change of ownership is often accompanied by increased competition, owing to the simultaneous granting of one or more mobile telephone licences and in some cases a second fixed licence. In Côte d'Ivoire, for example, connection costs dropped by 20 per cent following the privatisation of CI-Telecom, which coincided with the entry into the market of several competitors in mobile telephony and Internet services.

In contrast, privatisation in power and water has generally led to higher tariffs because the high sunk costs involved have constrained the liberalisation of these sectors. Moreover, since it had been common practice to subsidise electricity and water tariffs, many holders of concession and lease agreements have had to re-adjust tariffs to cost-recovering levels subsequent to privatisation. In many cases (e.g. Uganda, Zimbabwe and Zambia), tariffs have been raised before the actual privatisation in order to reduce the companies' financing gap and to attract strategic buyers.

In other cases, price increases have been attributable to badly monitored price regulation systems, such as cost-plus pricing. One way of overcoming the problem of information asymmetry (where the regulator does not have accurate information on the costs of suppliers) has been the adoption of rules for concession and lease bidding under which only the bidder offering service at the lowest price may be selected. Another instrument to limit tariff increases has been the adoption of price cap systems.

It should be noted, however, that despite the adverse impact of tariff increases, consumers have generally benefited from improvements in quality after privatisation. The reduction of distribution and transmission losses and the elimination of blackouts and brownouts appear to have more than offset increases in prices.

More rarely, privatisation has also led to tariff reduction in water and electricity. A good illustration is the case of Société d'Energie et d'Eau du Gabon (SEEG), where the awarding of a concession contract in 1997 to Veolia (alias Vivendi Water) brought decreases in the price of both electricity and water services. Such decreases were made possible by a well-designed concession contract that clearly specified the quality requirements and coverage targets expected from the private investor, combined with a preparatory restructuring phase that lasted about ten years.

Finally, some privatisation methods may well be consistent with a policy of subsidisation if the provision of public services at a reasonable price cannot be fully profitable. In the utilities sector, this would require clear and enforceable concession contracts that commit the concessionaire to supply services for the poor in exchange for an explicit or implicit subsidy. In turn, of course, this requires a transparent privatisation procedure and the implementation of an enforceable regulatory framework.

Labour Market Impact

The actual impact of privatisation on employment is difficult to assess, owing to the lack of accurate figures on pre- and post-privatisation employment. In general, privatisation is perceived to lead to job cuts in the short run, and this perception has caused massive protests by trade unions, which are the most vehement opponents of privatisation.

The available evidence on employment, however, is less clear-cut. The restructuring of previously overstaffed SOEs generally leads in the short run to redundancies, which in turn imply rising unemployment: SOEs are privatised to restore their economic efficiency, and cutting redundant staff is a necessary preliminary step. Otherwise, in such cases of initial overstaffing, the privatisation cannot meet its objectives.

The long-term impact is uncertain. The evidence for competitive sectors suggests that after registering a sometimes significant decrease in the year of privatisation, employment generally stabilises and then begins to trend upward in the two years following the launch of a privatisation plan. Examples of this pattern occurred in Tanzania and Mozambique.

Assessing the long-term impact of privatisation on employment is more challenging when considering the power and water sectors. In public utilities, large-scale retrenchments became imperative in order to lower costs and boost productivity, as the combination of considerable overstaffing and insufficient training to keep staff up to date seriously constrained efficiency gains. Job redundancies have been particularly severe in the electric power sector, as water has mostly remained under strong public control.

124

To soften the impact on employment, some national authorities have become more attentive to job preservation during the privatisation process. In Zambia and Burkina Faso, for instance, the retention of existing staff became an explicit criterion with which private investors had to comply. In the case of the privatised water company of Guinea, employees have been redeployed in subcontractor companies.

Where the remaining manpower in privatised companies is concerned, privatisation seems to have improved labour practices and led to increases in wages, as exemplified by the privatisation of CI-telecom in Côte d'Ivoire.

The Utilities Sector and Poverty

In Africa, access to public services is usually restricted to a minority of the population. Nearly 600 million people, or about 74 per cent of the total African population, have no access to electricity, and close to 300 million people are without access to safe water. Yet increased provision of drinking water is crucial to the improvement of health conditions and quality of life, and access to electricity is a major determinant of household productivity. For instance, electric light extends the day, providing additional time to study or work. Efficient and affordable energy services may also dramatically improve the health of the poor. Refrigeration allows local clinics to keep medicines on hand; modern cook stoves may save women and children from daily exposure to noxious cooking fumes. The utilities sector thus plays a crucial role in poverty alleviation policies.

Not all households can be connected to electricity and water distribution networks, particularly in rural areas and small towns, because low population density precludes economies of scale and raises the cost of extending networks to prohibitive levels. In urban areas, however, African states have done much to broaden access to safe water. During the 1980s, 120 million people were granted such access. This is certainly one of the few areas in which African governments have achieved commendable results, according to UNICEF. Much less has been achieved in terms of broadening access to electricity, although state intervention has been generally as frequent as in the water sector.

In sum, the evidence suggests that state management of utilities has been largely disappointing in the past, while privatisation accompanied by proper regulation seems to have proved a valuable alternative, ensuring increased access for consumers and overall improvements in quality.

The case of telecommunications is an outstanding example of how privatisation has improved the coverage of public services. In particular, the evidence shows that privatisation brings broader access when it is accompanied by the simultaneous introduction of competition and proper regulation, as demonstrated by the case of Sonatel in Senegal, where the presence of a proper regulatory framework and competition led to a substantial extension of telephone networks.

A credible regulatory framework, backed by strong political commitment, is also crucial to improving access in the power and water sectors. In absence of proper regulation, profit-maximising behaviour has led privatised companies to keep investments below the necessary levels, with the result that rural communities and the urban poor were further marginalised in terms of access to electric power and water supply. One way to overcome the difficulties linked to the marginalisation of certain categories of consumers would be to include, in the licences of concessionaires and private power distributors, specific targets for electrification of rural communities and poor urban neighbourhoods, which could be part of the minimum requirement for licence renewal. Another option that has proved to increase the electrification of rural communities and urban poor in developed countries is to sell off the distribution end in smaller entities rather than in its entirety.

The investments that would be needed to supply adequate quantities and qualities of public services to all households are of course very large, and will not be undertaken soon in Africa, with or without privatisation. The available evidence does suggest, however, that improvements in access are more likely when public services are managed by effectively regulated private companies rather than by the state. Nevertheless, increasing the number of households with access to these public services implies massive investment, both in production capacity and in network extension. These are long-term investments, and their viability depends in part on households' capacity to pay. To enhance access and design strategies to extend services to the poor, it is necessary to understand how much consumers are actually willing to pay and the constraints they face (in terms of access to credit, for instance). What is needed is a comprehensive strategy to co-ordinate the policies and programmes through which micro-credit, technology uptake and capacity building can take place. The formation of a well-balanced partnership between private operators, the government, customers and international lenders may be instrumental in improving access for the poor.

Annex 1

The Database

The World Bank's African Privatization Database was adopted as the main source for this analysis in preference to *African Development Indicators* because the latter records values that are not consistent with the information coming from other sources. The information used to complete and update the World Bank database comes mainly from the "Questionnaire on Privatisations" collected on-site by the *African Economic Outlook* team of the OECD Development Centre, working in collaboration with the African Development Bank. The results were also cross-checked against the estimates of Nellis (2003), covering the 1991-2001 period.

The questionnaires collected in the field, combined with information from various media sources as well as the most recently published papers on the subject, enabled us to improve considerably the sometimes very incomplete information reported by the World Bank for countries such as Burkina Faso, Cameroon, Gabon, Mali, Mozambique, South Africa, Zambia and Zimbabwe. For these countries, the ratio of "detailed" transactions was raised from sometimes less than 30 per cent to often more than 80 per cent (the methodology used for extrapolating the missing data is reported in Annex 2).

The cross-checking analysis also helped us to ignore non-detailed transactions that did not correspond to actual privatisations in the year mentioned but had been inserted in the World Bank database simply because they had appeared in the Letter of Intent of the country concerned, and that consequently sometimes led to double counting of privatisation transactions. However, when the decision to privatise coincided with the restructuring of the company (commonly seen as the first step in the privatisation process), we kept the information reported by the World Bank[1]. For instance, this was the case for Union Centrafricaine des Textiles (UCATEX), which is reported to have been "liquidated" in 1989 and privatised in 1993. Conversely, cross-checking enabled us to add detailed transactions that had actually taken place but had not been mentioned in the database. In Burkina Faso, for example, the sale of 50 per cent of the Societe Sucrière de la Comoe (SOSUCO) for a total amount of $6.2 million in 1998 was not recorded, while this privatisation is today seen as a great success.

The database is based on the three following technical assumptions:

1. All reported transactions involving a sale of assets or shares (however small) or the formal yielding of management control (as through a management contract) are included in the World Bank Africa Privatization Database. Hence, the term "privatisation" is used generically to include all of the following: the sale or disposal of some or all of the assets of public enterprises, the sale of government-owned shares in enterprises, reduction in the equity percentage held by a government through share dilutions or through transfer of enterprise assets to a new joint venture, liquidations, leases, concessions and management contracts. Each step of the privatisation of a company is reported (for example, a sale of block of shares to a core investor and a subsequent initial public offering). For countries like Mozambique, however, where formerly state-owned enterprises were split up into small entities before being privatised, the process is considered to be a single privatisation transaction. For Angola, the Africa Privatization Database reported 250 transactions on which no information was available. Owing to the lack of coherent information, such transactions have not been taken into account in our database. This prevented us from misleadingly presenting Angola as the country with the second largest number of transactions in the Southern Africa region.

2. In line with the World Bank database, sale proceeds of less than $10 000 are reported to be equal to zero, although this can lead to under-estimation of total sale proceeds. We also assumed the sale value to be equal to zero whenever the transaction value in the case of a liquidation, lease, concession or management contract was not reported. This often occurs in the case of liquidations and management contracts, where the government usually pays the new management team (and not the contrary). For instance, under the management contract signed between the Tanzanian government and the South African engineering firm NETGroup Solutions in April 2002 for running the Tanzania Electricity Supply Company (TANESCO), NETGroup Solutions will be paid a $2.6 million management fee for its first two years of management services. In the case of concessions and leases, the unique nature of each contract makes it too difficult (and risky) to extrapolate any transaction value.

3. In the World Bank database, amounts that are reported do not always correspond to what has actually been paid to governments and/or to privatisation agencies, which can lead to an over-estimation of sale proceeds. In South Africa, for instance, the privatisation in 1997 of SunAir, a small airline based in Johannesburg, was supposed to involve a cash payment of R40 million ($8.7 million). A down payment of R20 million ($4.3 million) was made at the time of sale, and the remainder of the sale price was to be paid out of improved cash flows. However, the airline became insolvent only a year after privatisation, and the outstanding sum was never paid. There can thus be a substantial discrepancy between the amounts initially announced and those that actually accrue to government. Whenever detected, such misreporting was modified in the database. This discrepancy between the official price and the amount paid justifies the use of the term "sale value" in the World Bank database, since "proceeds" might imply the value of amounts actually paid. In practice, and more specifically in the case of lease or concession contracts where fees are paid on a yearly basis, deals are structured so that new investors may acquire assets or shares on deferred terms.

Our methodology enabled us to obtain consistent results for the number and sale value of privatisation transactions to end 2002 and to compare them with existing data from *African Development Indicators 2002* (data available to end 2000) and from the recent survey by Nellis (2003; data available to end 2001).

Table AI.1 shows that, compared to our estimations and to Nellis (2003), the *African Development Indicators* overestimate both the number of privatisations and their sale value. More surprisingly, our statistics show both a greater number of privatisations and lower sale values than do Nellis's data. The detailed country data are reported in Annex 2.

There are two main reasons for the discrepancies with Nellis's sale values. First, as our analysis sets the value of transactions below $10 000 at zero, we may have missed some proceeds reported by Nellis. His statistics are derived from the compilation and updating of various databases, including not only the World Bank Africa Region Privatization Database, but also the *World Development Indicators*, IMF staff country reports and data collected by Campbell and Bhatia (1998). Some discrepancies may also stem from Nellis's attempts to extrapolate sale values for privatisations in the water and power sectors when these values were not officially reported.

More specifically, differences in **Central Africa** are mainly due to our reporting of greater privatisation sale values in Burundi ($19.8 million as against $4 million in Nellis, 2003), Central African Republic ($18.45 million as

Table A1.1. **Number of Privatisations and Sale Proceeds:**
A Comparison with *African Development Indicators* (2002) and Nellis (2003)

| | To end 2000 | | | | To end 2001 | | | | To end 2002 (authors' estimation) | | |
| | Number | | Value ($ million) | | Number | | Value ($ million) | | Number | | Value ($ million) |
	Authors' estimation	ADI[a] data	Authors' estimation	ADI[a] data	Authors' estimation	Nellis[b] data	Authors' estimation	Nellis[b] data	Exc. pending	Pending	
Central Africa	226	323	366	139	230	215	401	310	232	112	401
Eastern Africa	594	870	1 582	889	600	593	1 637	1 269	604	65	1 657
Western Africa	788	1 046	2 250	2 467	803	643	2 635	3 136	818	123	2 807
Southern Africa	865	1 292	3 181	3 856	873	819	3 309	4 397	881	32	3 951
TOTAL	2 473	3 531	7 378	7 351	2 506	2 270	7 982	9 112	2 535	332	8 816

a. ADI: *African Development Indicators*, 2002.
b. Data as reported in Nellis (2003).

against $0) and in Gabon ($65.18 million as against $0). In the case of Burundi, we increased the amount reported by the World Bank Africa Region Privatization Database by the sale value of the full divestiture of Air Burundi, using the privatisation of Lesotho Airways as a reference ($8 million). For the Central African Republic, the sale of a 40 per cent stake in the telecom company SOCATEL in 1990 to France Télécom is estimated at about $13 million on the basis of similar transactions in Niger, Republic of Congo and Guinea. For Gabon, official sources report the sale of a 51 per cent stake in the railway Office du Chemin de Fer Transgabonais (OCTRA) and of a 20-year concession for a total value of $31.30 million in 1999, while the full divestiture of Cimgabon (the country's only cement company, with three plants producing 210 000 tonnes), is reported to have amounted to $22 million the same year.

In **Eastern Africa**, we estimate greater privatisation amounts for Madagascar ($49.68 million versus $16.9 million), Uganda ($208.98 million versus $174 million), Sudan ($111.38 million versus $0) and Tanzania ($554.27 million versus $287 million). Regarding Madagascar, Nellis (2003) apparently does not take into account the full divestiture of the petroleum company SOLIMA, which was sold for $36 million in 2001. In Sudan, two substantial privatisations occurred in 1993: the full divestiture of the Sudan Commercial Bank and the National Mining Company, reported to have amounted to $12.43 million and $5.83 million respectively by the World Bank Privatization Database. In addition, we estimated the sale of 43 per cent of the telecom company Sudatel at $464.50 million on the basis of the initial capital ($150 million), which was increased to $250 million after privatisation. This was followed in 2001 by the flotation of an additional 7 per cent stake estimated at around $10 million by official sources. Finally, Nellis seems to have considerably underestimated the sale values for Tanzania, since according to the World Bank Privatization Database a mere ten transactions (of a total of around 200) already represent a total sale value of $285.53 million (of which $120 million stemmed from the privatisation of a 35 per cent stake in Tanzania Telecommunications Company in 2001). In contrast, we obtain lower sales amounts for Kenya ($248.86 million versus $381 million) and Ethiopia ($203.3 million versus $410 million). In the case of Kenya, Nellis records only two more transactions than we do, which hardly justifies the $132 million difference between our respective sale value estimates. Where Ethiopia is concerned, the inconsistency between our data and those of Nellis is even more blatant: we record the same number of transactions (ten), but our estimate (which is close to that of the World Bank database) is twice as high.

While our results are higher for Central and Eastern Africa, they are lower in the case of Western and Southern Africa. Nellis's estimates for **Western Africa** are higher than ours by $454 million. The divergences mainly concern three countries: Senegal ($217.14 million as against $415 million), Côte d'Ivoire ($423.64 million as against $622 million) and Nigeria ($528 million as against $893 million). The striking difference in the respective figures for Senegal is mainly attributable to the fact that we cancelled the proceeds resulting from the privatisation of a 33 per cent stake in Sénélec, as they were reimbursed following the re-nationalisation of the company.

The largest regional discrepancy ($1.1 billion) between the two samples arises in the case of **Southern Africa** and is mainly due to South Africa ($1.87 billion in our database as against $3.15 billion in Nellis's). This difference may be due to Nellis's extrapolation of future sales that actually occurred in 2002, such as the sale of 20 per cent of the cellular network operator M-Cell to the Dutch group Ice Finance for $475 million in January 2002.

Note

1. The World Bank considers the first step of the restructuring as a "liquidation" transaction and the second one as the actual privatisation.

Annex 2

Methodology Used to Extrapolate Missing Data

Sale Value Extrapolation for Privatised Enterprises in the Competitive Sectors

Where enterprises in the competitive sectors were privatised and the sale amounts not reported, we extrapolated the sale value on the basis of similar transactions carried out in similar sectors and countries.

Countries were thus classified in four groups according to size, measured as the average value of their gross domestic product at factor cost over a ten-year period (1990-2000), as reported in *African Development Indicators 2002* (World Bank). The following classification was obtained:

South Africa is considered a "special" case with an average GDP of $138 billion and 100 per cent of transactions detailed.

For countries where more than 50 per cent of transactions were detailed (the majority of countries), we extrapolated the sale amounts on the basis of detailed transactions conducted in the same sector and the same country. In Uganda, for instance, 15 privatisations were carried out in the "tourism/hotels" sector, with the following breakdown of privatisation methods:

—   10 privatisations through competitive sale of assets (AC): detailed;

—   2 privatisations through joint ventures (JV): detailed;

—   2 privatisations through competitive sale of shares (SC): not detailed;

—   1 privatisation through direct sale of shares (SD): not detailed.

Table A2.1. **Ranking of Countries by Extrapolation**

Group 1: Avg. < 1E+09	Reference country	Percentage of detailed transactions (after cross-checking)	GDP at factor cost
Burundi	X	80	9.35E+08
Cape Verde	X	55	3.74E+08
Gambia	X	60	3.34E+08
Guinea-Bissau	X	70	2.20E+08
Lesotho	Burundi	30	7.82E+08
Mauritania	X	80	9.24E+08
São Tomé and Principe	Cape Verde	30	4.09E+07
Sierra Leone	o	0	9.34E+08
Group 2: 1E+09 ≤ Avg. ≤ 3.5E+09	Reference country	Percentage of detailed transactions (after cross-checking)	GDP at factor cost
Benin	X	80	1.84E+09
Burkina Faso	X	85	2.10E+09
Central African Republic	Benin, Mali Burkina Faso	0	1.05E+09
Chad	X	80	1.40E+09
Congo, Rep.	Benin, Mali, Burkina Faso	20	2.40E+09
Guinea	Benin, Mali, Burkina Faso	30	3.41E+09
Madagascar	X	100	2.96E+09
Malawi	X	100	1.29E+09
Mali	X	100	2.21E+09
Mozambique	X	100	2.16E+09
Niger	X	70	1.87E+09
Rwanda	Malawi	30	1.67E+09
Togo	X	60	1.21E+09
Zambia	X	85	3.34E+09

Group 3: 4E+09 ≤ Avg. ≤ 6.5E+09	Reference country	Percentage of detailed transactions (after cross-checking)	GDP at factor cost
Angola	Ethiopia	0	5.73E+09
Ethiopia	X	100	5.35E+09
Gabon	X	90	4.58E+09
Ghana	X	80	5.66E+09
Senegal	X	90	4.10E+09
Sudan	Ethiopia	33	6.32E+09
Tanzania	X	60	4.79E+09
Uganda	X	80	4.90E+09
Zimbabwe	X	100	6.24E+09

Group 4: Avg. ≥ 7E+09	Reference country	Percentage of detailed transactions (after cross-checking)	GDP at factor cost
Cameroon	X	80	8.45E+09
Congo, Dem. Rep.	o	0	6.96E+09
Côte d'Ivoire	X	90	8.90E+09
Kenya	X	100	7.39E+09
Nigeria	X	100	2.68E+10

To fill the gap in our information on privatisations conducted through SD and SC, we used the average value of a 1 per cent share reported for detailed transactions carried out using the AC and JV methods. We then calculated the sale value by multiplying this 1 per cent average share by the number of shares privatised through the SC and SD transactions.

For countries where fewer than 50 per cent of transactions were detailed (Lesotho, Sao Tome & Principe, Central African Republic, Republic of Congo, Guinea, Rwanda, Angola and Sudan), we selected a "reference country" belonging to the same group and similar in terms of size and/or historical background. For instance, some privatisations in Guinea were extrapolated on the basis of the average value of a 1 per cent share in similar sectors in Mali, Burkina Faso and Benin. No transaction values were calculated in the case of Sierra Leone and the Democratic Republic of Congo, since no "real" privatisations seem to have occurred in these countries. The only transactions recorded are liquidations/restructuring, leases and management contracts, which do not seem to have brought in much in the way of sale proceeds.

Sale Value Extrapolation for Natural Monopolies

The rule used for competitive sectors was not systematically applied in transactions in "strategic" sectors such as: air transport, telecommunications, water and power, owing to the risk of seriously overestimating the amounts that actually accrued to the country. For instance, if we had calculated the privatisation of Companhia Santomense de Telecommunicacoes (CST) in Sao Tome & Principe solely on the basis of the privatisation of Cabo Verde Telecom, we would have found a sale value of $25 million, whereas the transaction actually amounted to only $1 million according to the International Labour Organisation.

Our initial objective was thus to make the most of available information sources and to avoid debatable extrapolations. For three specific transactions, we extrapolated the sale value from the capital of the company. In the case of Air Senegal, 51 per cent of which was sold to Royal Air Maroc, we knew that the company's capital stock amounted to about $10 million and hence estimated the sale value of the transaction at $5.1 million. The same method was applied to the sale of Uganda Clays Ltd in 1999 and that of Sudatel (Sudan's Telecom company) in 1994.

When accounting data were not available, the extrapolation was performed by reference to highly comparable transactions (in terms of the size and sector of the company concerned). The details of these extrapolations appear below.

Air Transport

In the case of air transport, we extrapolated the sale value of shares of Gambia Airways, Air Mauritanie and Burundi Airways on the basis of the privatisation of Lesotho Airways, which appears to have been very similar in size. This led us to assume that 60 per cent of Gambia Airways was sold for $4.88 million in 1994, that 65 per cent of Air Mauritanie was worth $5.24 million in 2000 and that 100% of Air Burundi amounted to about $8.33 million in 1997 (an 80 per cent share of Lesotho Airways was sold for $6.5 million in 1997).

Similarly, we used the privatisation of Air Mali SA after the company's liquidation/restructuring in 1992 (amounting to $11.5 million) as a reference for estimating the sale value of Air Burkina. We found a sale value of almost $5 million for the 40 per cent stake in Air Burkina sold to the Aga Khan Group on 21 February 2001.

Petroleum/Gas Distribution

In the case of petroleum/gas distribution, we used the sale of 20 per cent of the assets of Société d'Importation et de Commercialisation des Produits Petroliers (SICOPP) in Burundi in 1992 as a yardstick for assessing the sale value of similar companies in Cape Verde, Guinea-Bissau and Sao Tome & Principe. In Cape Verde, 65 per cent of Empresa Nacional de Combustíveis (Enacol), a company specialised in the distribution of fuel products, was sold in 1997 to the Portuguese firm Petrogal and Angola's state-owned oil company Sonangol; 30 per cent of Sodigas (the company in charge of gas distribution) was also sold in 1997. In Guinea-Bissau, a 90 per cent stake in Distribudora de Combustiveis e Lubrificantes (Dicol) was sold to Shell and Petromar. In 1999, the Sao Tome government sold 49 per cent of Empresa Nacional de Combusiveis (ENCO), including a 40 per cent stake to Sonangol.

Telecommunications

When the similarities between the reference transactions and the ones for which we lacked information were less clear-cut, we increased the number of transactions used for reference. For instance, we assessed the sale value of a 70 per cent share of Lesotho Telecom — sold to Mountain Kingdom Communications, a consortium led by Mauritius Telecom, South Africa's Eskom Entreprises and Zimbabwe's Econet Wireless International — on the basis of the privatisation of Mauritel, the Mauritanian telecom company, of Cabo Verde Telecom, of CST (the Sao Tome telecom company) and Guiné-Telecom (Guinea-Bissau). Similarly, the sale value of the 40 per cent stake in Socatel, the telecom company of the Central African Republic, sold in 1990 to France Câble & Radio, was extrapolated on the basis of the sale of a 67 per cent stake in the Republic of Congo's Office National des Postes et Télécommunications (ONPT) to US-Atlantic Tele-Network in 1997, of a 51 per cent share of Société Nigerienne de Télécommunications (Sonitel) to Z.T.E Corporation China Right Com in 2001 and of 60 per cent of Soltegui (Guinea's telecom company) to Telekom Malaysia in 1996.

Power/Water Sectors

Power and water are the only two sectors for which no values were extrapolated. We were unable to establish any consistent rule for these sectors owing to the nature of the privatisation methods applied (management, lease or concession contracts rather than outright sales of shares or assets). Therefore, sale values are presented only for a limited number of transactions.

To conclude the presentation of our methodology, we describe our treatment of privatisation/renationalisation episodes. To date, such reversals have occurred in five countries, of which only Uganda sold a renationalised company back to the market.

In **Senegal**, following the cancellation in September 2000 of the privatisation of the power company Sénélec (a 33 per cent stake in which had been sold to a consortium led by Elyo/Hydro-Québec), the government had to reimburse CFAF 44 billion (about $62 million) to the buyer. It subsequently entered into negotiations with Vivendi/ONE in July 2001, and then with AES in July 2002, but both deals fell through. We therefore record no sale value for the first privatisation of Sénélec in 1998. In principle, we could have recorded a loss for the government, since the failed privatisation is supposed to have cost an additional CFAF 67 billion to restore Sénélec's cash position (CFAF 41 billion) and to re-capitalise the company (CFAF 26 billion).

In **Guinea**, the same events occurred in both the water and power sectors. In the former, after the 2000 breakdown of an *affermage* contract concluded between the state and a consortium led by SAUR and Vivendi in 1989, the state decided to renationalise the water company temporarily through the creation of a new state-owned company,: the Société des Eaux de Guinée (SEG). Similarly, in the power sector, an *affermage* contract between the state and a consortium led by EDF/Hydro-Québec broke down, and a new state-owned enterprise, Electricité de Guinée (EDG), was formed after the re-nationalisation of the sector.

South Africa is the third country to have implemented a partial re-nationalisation. In June 1999, Swissair became the strategic partner of South African Airways (SAA), acquiring 20 per cent of the national carrier for R1.4 billion ($202 million). Swissair paid an additional R48 million ($7 million) for an option to buy a further 10 per cent. The acquisition agreement was formally signed on 19 November 1999. In 2002, however, after months of negotiations, a team of government officials and officers of Transnet (the state-owned transport company holding the majority stake in SAA) secured a deal to repurchase, at a bargain price, the 20 per cent stake in SAA sold to Swissair three years before. The repurchase agreement did not, however, lead to an outright cancellation of the amount formerly paid by Swissair: in contrast to what happened in Senegal, where the re-nationalisation occasioned a heavy loss for the government, the South African state, through SAA's parent company Transnet, received R1 billion (about $145 million). Actually, Transnet bought the SAA shares back at a significant discount, paying just R382.5 million, which was equal to their fair value less a 15 per cent default discount stipulated in the shareholders' agreement.

In **Zambia**, the government re-nationalised Konkola Copper Mines (KCM), Zambia's largest mining company, which accounted for about two-thirds of the country's copper production in 2002. KCM was acquired in March 2000 by a consortium led by the Anglo-South African mining firm, the Anglo-American Corporation. The acquisition took place when KCM's asset value had dropped greatly owing to the obsolescence of the plant and the slump in copper prices (the acquisition price amounted to $90 million, as compared to an offer of $165 million received in 1998). Privatisation of the mines was delayed because they were considered national treasures, and there was no agreement within the government and mining circles regarding their disposal. Delayed privatisation and lack of investment led to unproductive, inefficient and overstaffed entities, characterised by bad management and corruption. In January 2002, after incurring substantial losses ($108 million in the two years to December 2001), Anglo-American announced its decision to pull out of the mining activities. In August 2002, Anglo-American divested completely, agreeing to leave its management team in place, and providing $30 million and a loan of $26.5 million to keep operations running at KCM until new investors could be found. The government has undertaken to run the mines until a new strategic investor is found.

Finally, in **Uganda**, the Uganda Commercial Bank has been reprivatised through the sale of an 80 per cent stake to Standard Bank Investment Corporation (Stanbic) of South Africa in February 2002, for a total of about $19 million. The bank had been renationalised in 2001 when the sale of a similar stake to the Malaysian company Westmont proved to be a swindle and was finally condemned and cancelled by international donors.

Annex 3

Pending Privatisations in Utilities

Pending Privatisations in Telecommunications as of March 2003

Country	Company	Comments
Benin	Société Béninoise des Télécommunications (SOBETEL)	Privatisation planned for 2003, but the government has not yet decided on the method of privatisation
Burkina Faso	Office National des Télécommunications (ONATEL)	The decision to privatise was made in 1998, but the process was launched only in 2001 and the finalisation of contracts started in May 2003. The ownership shares should be as follows: - 34 per cent: strategic investor; - 20 per cent: flotation; - 6 per cent: employees; - 40 per cent: government and private investors. It is planned to increase the stake of the strategic investor by 10 per cent by 2007 and by an additional 7 per cent by 2009.
Burundi	ONATEL	Burundi's public privatisation office plans to sell 51 per cent of its shares to private companies (foreign strategic investors). The state would retain 35 per cent of the corporation's share capital, while the remaining 14 per cent would be split between the public and ONATEL employees. A call for tenders for pre-selection of bidders was launched in February 2001, but as of mid-2003 the company had not been sold.
Cameroon	Cameroon Telecommunications (CAMTEL)	Telcel was provisionally selected to take over Camtel (fixed-line telephony) but withdrew after its partner, Orascom, preferred to look elsewhere. The replacement bidder, Mont Cameroun, submitted an updated tender in February 2002 but subsequently failed to confirm its bid ending the procedure. The government asked Ondéo-Service (formerly Lyonnaise des Eaux) to amend its bid for SNEC (water company), which had been deemed inadequate. The firm submitted an updated tender in December 2001, and negotiations to draw up a contract are under way. These are likely to be difficult, given the strong criticisms encountered by other privatisation deals.
Central African Rep.	Socatel	It is planned to sell a portion of the state's 60 per cent interest (the remaining 40 per cent is owned by France Câble). Discussions were held in 2003 to determine the percentage that the government should privatise. SOCATEL has the monopoly on fixed-line telephone service and also controls the wireless telecom company.

Chad	Office National des Postes et Télécommunications (ONPT)	The privatisation process is under consideration.
Congo, Rep. of	Société d'Exploitation des Télécommunications	
Ethiopia	Ethiopian Telecommunications Corporation (ETC)	The Ethiopian government started planning the privatisation of ETC in 2001. In 1999, Price Waterhouse was contracted to draft tender documents, conduct an asset evaluation and develop strategies for the privatisation. Tilahun Kebde, General Manager of the Telecommunication Agency, said an international tender would be launched soon.
Gabon	Gabon Télécom	The post and telecommunications authority was split in two in August 2001, with Gabon Poste set for restructuring and Gabon Télécom for privatisation. The short list of firms bidding for the latter was announced in July 2002, with a deadline for bids at the end of September. Gabon Telecom includes the fixed-line phone system and the Libertis subsidiary, which runs the country's biggest mobile phone network. The privatisation of Gabon Télécom has been subject to a number of delays.
Gambia	Gamtel	
Guinea-Bissau	Guiné Telecom	Portugal Telecom SA (PT) declared that the government of Guinea-Bissau has unilaterally rescinded the concession contract for public telecommunications services it had established with PT. According to PT, Guiné Telecom, in which PT has a 51 per cent stake, while the government holds 49 per cent, had been operating under a 20-year concession contract since 1989. No explanation was given for the decision to rescind the contract. PT said the move would have no economic impact on PT, because its financial investment in Guiné Telecom is fully covered by provisions.
Kenya	Telkom Kenya	In January 2000, after weeks of delays, Kenya agreed to sell a 49 per cent interest in its fixed-line telecom monopoly. Mount Kenya Telecommunications, a consortium involving the Zimbabwe-based group ECONET Wireless International, the Dutch group Royal KPN NV and the South African firm Eskom, had agreed to pay $305 million for the stake in Telkom Kenya. However, the privatisation was finally postponed in November 2002, and was supposed to get started again after the general election. The process should be continued, especially since President Kibaki seriously criticised parastatals in January 2003.

Madagascar	Telekom Malagasy	Planned since 1996, the privatisation of Madagascar's public operator Telekom Malagasy (TELMA) began only in June 2001, when the government's privatisation committee published in the local press an invitation to tender for 36 per cent of the company. In December 2001, Distacom was selected to purchase 34 per cent of Telecom Malagasy, beating out France Télécom. However, the signature of the final agreement transferring TELMA to Distacom, scheduled for 18 December 2002, has not taken place. In May 2003, President Marc Ravalomanana resumed the privatisation process, which had stalled under the previous regime. The TELMA privatisation is expected to be concluded by the end of the year, as Distacom and the state are negotiating the terms of the transfer.
Malawi	Malawi Telecommunications	The Commission commenced its remarketing of MTL with a request for expressions of interest (EoIs), which was published locally as well as internationally. By December 2002, seven EoIs were received and by February 2003, three consortia had been formed for the purpose of submitting technical and financial bids. The Commission and a technical steering committee opened and evaluated the technical proposals in June 2003. Press Corporation-CDC-Detecon and TCIL-Mahanagar Telekom-NICO have been asked to submit their financial bids by 20 June 2003. A minimum of 30 per cent of MTL is up for sale. The strategic investor will be allowed to subscribe, simultaneously, for further shares up to a limit of 80 per cent of MTL. As a demonstration of its commitment to the process, the government has agreed to cede management control.
Mali	Société des Télécommunications du Mali (Sotelma)	The government chose to liberalise the tele-communications sector before privatising Sotelma. A second operating licence, for fixed, mobile and international phone lines, was awarded to France Télécom in August 2002, with operations expected to begin at the end of December. The authorities are dealing with the restructuring needed for disposal of Sotelma, (including an audit of the accounts and the investments made for the Africa Nations Cup).
Mozambique	Telecommunications de Mocambique (TDM)	In January 1999, the government began drafting reform legislation for the telecommunications sector, which is likely to open the sector somewhat to private investment and competition. Thus far, TDM has entered into several joint ventures, but privatisation is not expected in the short term.

Nigeria	Nigerian Telecommunication Limited (Nitel)	In March 2003, the government concluded plans to float its 20 per cent equity in Nitel on the Nigerian Stock Exchange. Moroeover, the National Council on Privatisation (NCP) finalised arrangements to launch the N10 billion Privatisation Share Purchase Loan Scheme (PSPLS) following the successful signing of a restructuring agreement with the management contractor.
Rwanda	Rwandatel	The privatisation of Rwandatel is part of a broader government policy for economic liberalisation, implemented since 2002. A strategic investor is expected to acquire 51 per cent, while 43 per cent will be reserved to Rwandan nationals, 5 per cent to employees and 1 per cent to the state. In mid-2002, the government recruited a consultant for the due diligence process.
Togo	Togo Telecom	Togo Telecom emerged from the split-up of the Office National des Postes in 1997, and was to be privatised in early 2001. The company has enjoyed several lines of credit, mainly for a telephone network extension project, raising the number of connections from 32 400 to 108 500 by the end of 2008.
Zambia	Zamtel	The privatisation of Zambia's national telecommunications services provider Zamtel is still on hold. The cabinet approved the sale of a 20 per cent interest. Further clarifications are awaited from the government. At present, Zamtel faces very limited competition from two cellular providers and a number of other authorised operators are providing Internet and pay phone services.
Zimbabwe	Tel-One	The privatisation of Tel-One expected in 2002 did not occur, owing to the government's failure to secure foreign bidders. In May 2002, the government short-listed four bidders — DeTeCon (Germany), Mauritius Telecom, MegaTel (a consortium of locally-based regional banks) and Mobile Systems International (the Netherlands) — to acquire the 30 per cent stake, but all have since lost interest, citing ever-escalating finance charges.

Pending Privatisations in Power

Country	Company	Comments
Mauritania	SOMELEC	After the sale of Air Mauritanie and Mauritel, the Mauritanian government had completed all the preparatory work in setting regulatory law and the bidding procedures to privatise the national electricity supplier SOMELEC in 2002. For reasons beyond the government's control, however, the sale has not been completed. Of the five multinational companies who qualified to bid on SOMELEC during the bid qualification phase in 2001, all but one had withdrawn by spring 2002. The apparent reason for these wholesale withdrawals has less to do with Mauritania or SOMELEC than with the severe disruptions in the financial status of many leading multinational power companies in the aftermath of the collapse of the US energy giant Enron in late 2001. The government and IMF have concluded that it is preferable to defer the sale of SOMELEC until a later time when market conditions for the potential bidders improve.
Burkina Faso	SONABEL	The privatisation process is reported to be at an advanced stage.
Malawi	Electricity Supply Corporation of Malawi (ESCOM)	In 1999, an Electricity Act established an independent regulatory body and incorporated ESCOM under the Companies Act. Since then, a debt restructuring initiated by the IMF has taken place, and the privatisation process is expected to start soon.
Mozambique	Electricidade de Moçambique (EDM)	Privatisation is planned, but is not expected to take place in the short term.
Zambia	Zambia Electricity Supply Company (ZESCO)	The IMF and World Bank recommend a management concession to improve the management of the power company. In 1999, a management contract had already been granted to Elyo/Lysa.
Central African Rep.	Energie centrafricaine (ENERCA)	In 2002, the World Bank and IMF called on the government to move faster in selecting private operators for ENERCA, SOCATEL and the water utility SNE.
Congo, Rep. of	Société Nationale d'Electricité (SNE)	Vivendi and Biwater were selected for the contract in 2002, but it is not yet known who won the tender.

146

Uganda	Uganda Electricity Distribution Company Ltd (UEDCL)	The Uganda Electricity Board has been divided into three companies: - Uganda Electricity Generation Company (UEGC): a concession was awarded to Eskom in 2002; - Uganda Electricity Distribution Company Ltd (UEDCL): Eskom and CDC Capital Ventures are the sole bidders for the UEDCL concession; - Uganda Electricity Transmission Company (UETC): will not be privatised.
Zimbabwe	Zimbabwe Electricity Supply Authority (ZESA)	The New Electricity Act in Zimbabwe provides for the establishment of a holding company, ZESA Ltd, with three subsidiaries responsible for generation, transmission and distribution. However, an outright privatisation of the Authority is not yet scheduled.
Nigeria	Nigerian Electric Power Authority (NEPA)	The company is currently being restructured.
Kenya	Kenya Power and Lighting Company (KPLC) and Kenya Electricity Generating Company (KenGen)	In July 2000, the World Bank urged Kenyan officials to set a specific timetable for the privatisation of KPLC and KenGen. As one of the pre-conditions for the privatisation process, a new electricity tariff was issued in June 2002.
South Africa	Eskom	A 30 per cent stake was scheduled for privatisation in 2003, and it is expected to be privatised soon.
Senegal	Société Nationale d'Electricité du Sénégal (Sénélec)	In Senegal, the cancellation in September 2000 of the privatisation of the power company Sénélec (a 33 per cent stake had been sold to a consortium led by Elyo/Hydro-Québec) entailed the reimbursement of CFAF 44 billion (about $62 million) that had been paid by the consortium, as well as the renationalisation of the company after the failure of negotiations with Vivendi/ONE in July 2001, and then with AES in July 2002.

Pending Privatisations in Water and Power

Country	Company	Comments
Gambia	National Water and Electricity Company (NAWEC)	NAWEC is the former electricity and water company GUC, the management of which had been contracted out to SOGEA under a lease contract in 1992 (unilaterally terminated in 1995 by the government).
Benin	Société Béninoise d'Eau et d'Electricité (SBEE)	The privatisation is highly recommended by the IMF and World Bank.
Guinea-Bissau	Electricidade e Agua da Guiné-Bissau (EAGB)	EAGB, due to very poor performance, needs a restructuring before being privatised.
São Tomé & Principe	Empresa da Agua e Electricidade (EMAE)	Since 2000, the IMF has been pushing the Sao Tome government to privatise nine public enterprises, including EMAE.
Rwanda	Electrogaz	In 2001, Rwanda's privatisation unit short-listed six multinational companies bidding to provide Electrogaz with new management. The firms are Eskom Entreprises of South Africa, SAUR International of France, a consortium of Lahmayer International and Hamburger Wasserwerke of Germany, a consortium comprising Manitoba Hydro and Roche Ltd of Canada, Tata Electric Supply Company of India and a consortium of four Belgian firms. The winner of the bid is not yet known.

148

Pending Privatisations in Water

Country	Company	Comments
Ghana	Ghana Water Company	According to Bayliss (2002), "bids have been invited for leases for the national water supply which has been divided into 2 'business units'. Bids are expected for the 2 leases. Business unit A covers the Greater Accra, Volta, Northern Upper East and Upper West regions. The contract to be awarded is for 30 years. Bidders are Northumbrian Water, Vivendi and SAUR. Business unit B covers the Central, Eastern, Western, Ashanti and Brong Ahafo regions. The lease is for 10 years. Bidders are Biwater, Nuon, Vivendi, Suez Lyonnaise and Skanska."
Nigeria	Lagos Water	The Lagos Water and Sanitation Project consisted of the following three major components: - a management and regulatory contract; - a contract for water and sewerage services in the Lagos Mainland zone; - a concession for water and sewerage services in Lekki and the islands zone. However, the privatisation process has been temporarily put on hold by the Nigerian government.
Burundi	National Water and Power Distribution and Production Company (REGIDESO)	Government is seeking a private operator under a lease contract for the national electricity company, REGIDESO. In February 2002, Good Governance and Privatisation Minister Didace Kiganahe reported that the privatisation was at an advanced stage.

Country	Company	Comments
Tanzania	Dar es Salaam Water and Sewerage Authority (DAWASA)	The IMF insisted on privatising DAWASA in 1997, but the process of selecting the private operator has been plagued by scandal and controversy. The first bidding process was stopped after two French companies, Saur International and Vivendi, were rejected. In 2002, the government said that the privatisation of DAWASA would be "done in two stages". Loans totalling $145 million will be committed during the first stage. DAWASA will then be leased to a private operator for ten years. Eight companies have made their submissions in the re-bid process, including three from France, Germany and the United Kingdom. After the first stage, "the privatisation status of DAWASA will then change from lease to concession", according to the Tanzanian water ministry. Privatising DAWASA is one of the conditions that must be satisfied if the country is to receive HIPC debt relief.
Cameroon	Société Nationale des Eaux du Cameroun (SNEC)	In May 2000, Suez Lyonnaise (now called Ondéo Service) announced that it had been selected as sole bidder to acquire the Cameroon government's 51 per cent stake in the public water company SNEC and a 20-year concession to operate the country's water provision system. Rapid privatisation of SNEC was required for Cameroon to qualify for debt relief from the World Bank and the IMF (Bayliss and Hall, 2000). However, the negotiations broke down in 2002, leading to the withdrawal of Suez, after it was reported that the price put forward was considered by the government to be too low.

Bibliography

ALHASSAN, A. (2003): Telecom regulation, the post-colonial state, and big business: the Ghanaian experience, *West Africa Review,* vol. 4.

ANDREASSON, B. (1998), *Privatisation in Sub-Saharan Africa: Has It Worked and What Lessons Can Be Learnt?,* Swedish Development Advisers, Gothenburg, Sweden.

APPIAH-KUBI, K. (2001), "State-owned Enterprises and Privatisation in Ghana", *Journal of Modern African Studies,* Vol. 39, No. 2.

ARIYO, A. AND A. JEROME (1999), "Privatization in Africa: An Appraisal", *World Development,* Vol. 27, No. 1.

AYOGU, M. (2001), *Debating 'Privatisation' of Network Utilities in South Africa,* University of Cape Town, South Africa.

AZAM, J.P., M. DIA AND T. N'GUESSAN (2002), "Telecommunications Sector Reform in Senegal", *Working Paper,* World Bank, Washington, D.C., September.

BAYLISS, K. (2002), "Privatisation and Poverty: The Distributional Impact of Utility Privatisation", Centre on Regulation and Competition, *Working Paper Series,* Paper No. 16, University of Manchester, January.

BAYLISS, K. (2001a), "Privatisation of Electricity Distribution: Some Economic, Social and Political Perspectives", Centre on Regulation and Competition, *Working Paper Series,* University of Manchester, April.

BAYLISS, K. (2001b), "Privatisation and the World Bank: A Flawed Development Tool", *Global Focus,* Vol. 13, June.

BAYLISS, K. (2001c), *Water Privatisation in Africa: Lessons from Three Case Studies,* PSIRU, University of Greenwich, May.

BAYLISS, K.AND D. HALL (2000), *Privatisation of Water and Energy in Africa,* A Report for Public Services International (PSI), PSIRU, University of Greenwich, London.

BAYLISS, K., HALL, D. AND E. LOBINA (2001), *Has Liberalisation Gone too Far?* A Review of the Issues in Water and Energy, Public Services International Research Unit, London.

BIRDSALL, N. AND J. NELLIS (2002), "Winners and Losers: Assessing the Distributional Impacts of Privatisation", Centre for Global Development, *Working Paper* No. 6, Washington, D.C., May.

BIRDSALL, N. AND J. NELLIS (2003), *The Distributional Impact of Privatisation*, Centre for Global Development, Washington, D.C., January.

BOUBAKRI, N. AND J.C. COSSET (1998), *Privatisation in Developing Countries: An Analysis of the Performance of Newly Privatised Firms*, World Bank, Washington, D.C., December.

BOUBAKRI, N. AND J.C. COSSET (2002), "Does Privatisation Meet the Expectations in Developing Countries? A Survey and Some Evidence from Africa", *Journal of African Economies*, Vol. 11, Spring.

CAMPBELL, W. AND A. BHATIA (1998), *Privatisation in Africa*, World Bank, Washington, D.C.

COGNEAU, D. (2002), *Colonisation, Schooling and Development in Africa: An Empirical Analysis*, DIAL, October.

COMMISSION DE PRIVATISATION (2000), "Bilan des privatisations au Burkina Faso, 1991-1999", Ministère du Commerce et de la Promotion de l'Entreprise et de l'Artisanat, Burkina Faso, October.

DAVIS, J., R. OSSOWSKI, T. RICHARDSON AND S. BARNETT (2000), "Fiscal and Macroeconomic Impact of Privatisation", *IMF Occasional Paper* No. 194, Washington, D.C.

GALIANI, S, P. GERTLER AND E. SCHARGRODSKY (2002), "Water for Life: The Impact of the Privatisation of Water Services on Child Mortality", *Working Paper*, Stanford University.

GUASH, J.L., J.J LAFFONT ET S. STRAUB (2002), *Renegotiation of Concession Contracts in Latin America*, World Bank, Washington, D.C.

GUISLAIN, P. AND M. KERF (1996), "Concessions — the Way to Privatise Infrastructure Sector Monopolies", *Public Policy for the Private Sector*, World Bank, Washington, D.C.

GUPTA, S., C. SHILLER AND H. MA (1999), "Privatisation, Social Impact, and Social Safety Nets", *IMF Working Paper*, No. 68, Washington, D.C.

HALL, D., K. BAYLISS AND E. LOBINA (2002), *Water Privatisation in Africa*, PSIRU, University of Greenwich, June.

HARSCH, E. (2000), "Privatization Shifts Gears in Africa", *Africa Recovery*, Vol. 14, No. 1.

ILO (INTERNATIONAL LABOUR OFFICE) (1998), *Managing the Privatisation and Restructuring of Public Utilities* (Water, Gas, Electricity), Geneva.

KAREKEZI, S. AND J. KIMANI (2002), *Status of Power Sector Reform in Africa: Impact on the Poor*, Afrepren.

KAYIZZI-MUGERWA, S. (2002), "Privatisation in Sub-Saharan Africa: On Factors Affecting Implementation", *WIDER Discussion Paper* No. 2002/12, January.

Kebede, B. (2002), *Poverty, Energy and Millennium Development Targets*, Afrepren, October.

Kerf, M. (2000), *Do State Holding Companies Facilitate Private Participation in the Water Sector? Evidence from Côte d'Ivoire, the Gambia, Guinea and Senegal*, World Bank, Washington, D.C.

Kikeri, S. (1999), "Labour Redundancies and Privatisation: What Should Governments Do?", *Public Policy for the Private Sector*, Note No. 174, World Bank Group, January.

Laffont, J.J. and T. N'Guessan (2002), "Telecommunications Reform in Côte d'Ivoire", *Working Paper*, World Bank, September.

Leroy, P., Y. Jammal and N. Gokgur (2002), *Impact of Privatisation in Côte d'Ivoire*, BIDE, July.

Mahboobi, L. (2002), "Recent Privatisation Trends in OECD Countries", *Financial Market Trends*, No. 82, OECD, Paris, June.

Makalou, O. (2001), *Escaping Poverty: Is Privatisation a Solution in Africa?*, CERDES, Mali.

Makalou, O. (1999), *Privatisation in Africa: A Critical Analysis*, World Bank, December.

Makonnen, D. (1999), "Broadening Local Participation in Privatisation of Public Assets in Africa", United Nations Economic Commission for Africa, *Working Paper Series*.

Ménard, C. and G. Clarke (2000), *Reforming Water Supply in Abidjan, Côte d'Ivoire: A Mild Reform in a Turbulent Environment*, World Bank, Washington, D.C.

Ménard, C., G. Clarke and A.M. Zuluaga (2000), *The Welfare Effects of Private Sector Participation in Urban Water Supply in Guinea*, World Bank, Washington, D.C.

Ménard, C. and Shirley, M. (1999), *Cities Awash: Reforming Urban Water Systems in Developing Countries*, World Bank, Development Research Group, Washington, D.C.

Mookherjee, D. and D. McKenzie (2002), "The Distributive Impact of Privatisation in Latin America: Evidence from Four Countries", *Working Paper*, Stanford University and Boston University.

Nellis, J. (2003), "Privatisation in Africa: What Has Happened? What Is to Be Done?", Centre for Global Development, *Working Paper* No. 25, February.

Odife, D. (2000), *Capital Market Development: The Road Ahead*, UNITAR, Document No. 13, Geneva, November.

Plane, P. (2001), "The Reform of Telecommunications in Sub-Saharan Africa", *Technical Papers* No. 174, OECD Development Centre, March.

Rosotto, C., M. Kerf and J. Rohlfs (1999), "Competition in Mobile Telecoms", *Public Policy for the Private Sector*, Note No. 184, World Bank Group, August.

Sheshinski, E. and L.F. López-Calva (1998), "Privatisation and Its Benefits: Theory and Evidence", CAER II, *Discussion Paper* No. 35, December.

Shirley, M., F. Tusubira, F. Gebreab and L. Haggarty (2002), "Telecommunications Reform in Uganda", *Working Paper,* World Bank, July.

Smith, P. (1997), "What the Transformation of Telecom Markets Means for Regulation", *Public Policy for the Private Sector* Note No. 121, World Bank, Washington, D.C.

Temu, A. and J. Due (1998), "The Success of Newly Privatised Companies: New Evidence from Tanzania", *Canadian Journal of Development Studies*, Vol. 19, No. 2.

Trémolet, S. (2002), "Multi-utilities and Access", *Public Policy for the Private Sector*, Note No. 248, World Bank Group, June.

Wallsten, S.J. (1999), "An Empirical Analysis of Competition, Privatisation and Regulation in Africa and Latin America", *Working Paper*, World Bank, Washington, D.C.

OECD PUBLICATIONS, 2, rue André-Pascal, 75775 PARIS CEDEX 16
PRINTED IN FRANCE
(41 2004 02 1 P) ISBN 92-64-02036-5 – No. 53365 2004